Peter Watkins is the Vicar of St N
West London. He has for many
the oddities of church life and a co   ...s about
it. He has a wide knowledge of chu.   ...story and has compiled a chronological survey of the history of the church in
London.

He is the author of numerous books, including the trilogy
Here's the Church, Here's the Year and *Here are the People,*
A Book of Prayer and *A Book of Animals.*

THE SOUL OF WIT

∾∾∾∾∾∾

*Eccentricity, absurdity
and other ecclesiastical treasures*

COMPILED BY
PETER WATKINS

CANTERBURY
PRESS
Norwich

© in this compilation Peter Watkins 2002

First published in 2002 by the Canterbury Press Norwich
(a publishing imprint of Hymns Ancient & Modern Limited,
a registered charity)
St Mary's Works, St Mary's Plain,
Norwich, Norfolk, NR3 3BH

www.scm-canterburypress.co.uk

All rights reserved. No part of this publication may be reproduced,
stored in a retrieval system, or transmitted,
in any form or by any means, electronic, mechanical,
photocopying or otherwise, without the prior permission of
the publisher, Canterbury Press

The editor has asserted his right under the
Copyright, Design and Patent Act, 1988, to be
identified as the Editor of this Work

British Library Cataloguing in Publication data

A catalogue record for this book is available
from the British Library

ISBN 1-85311-496-0

Typeset by Rowland Phototypesetting Ltd,
Bury St Edmunds, Suffolk
Printed and bound by Biddles Ltd, *www.biddles.co.uk*

CONTENTS

I am grateful for the help given by Gay Darwent in the preparation of this book.

For Susan

An Introduction:
The Language of Wit

Humour, and mirth, had place in all he writ:
He reconciled divinity and wit.
Dean Jonathan Swift on himself

So when the grave rebuke the merry
Let them remember Philip Neri
(Fifteen-fifteen to ninety-five),
Who was the merriest man alive,
Then, dying at eighty and a bit,
Became a saint by Holy Wit.
Phyllis McGinley on St Philip Neri,
a saint noted for his hilarity

Are we then to think of heaven as quite humourless, St.
Philip Neri and St. Thomas More never smiling again?
Ronald Knox in a letter to Miss Joyce Lambert, 1944

Man, please thy Maker and be merry
And give not for this world a cherry.
William Dunbar

A life without humour is neither healthy nor holy, human nor divine. The English masons and woodcarvers of cathedrals and parish churches did not suppose that Christian worship must be totally solemn. They placed comic figures and grotesque figures everywhere except in the very sanctuary. Grinning little devils are hidden under chancel seats on misericords. The Imp of Lincoln looks down on congregations in the cathedral with a comic eye. In one ecclesiastical carving the onlookers are holding their noses as Lazarus is raised from the dead.

It has been claimed that Satan fell by the force of gravity. The power of levity, on the other hand, is a characteristic of the greatest saints. They are humble enough to treat themselves lightly. They can laugh at themselves. They are not weighed down by the insanity of ponderous and pompous vanity. 'Angels can fly', remarked G. K. Chesterton, 'because they take themselves lightly.'

It is in this spirit that this anthology of humour within the Church is presented. It is reflected in the sayings of Christian wits, in verse, in anecdotes both historical and fictional, in comically curious facts, in prayers and graces, and in glimpses of the divine. It is something broader than a collection of jokes.

The wit and humour of this book are inclusive. There may be nothing intrinsically comic about a priest with a glass of wine or a cricket bat in his hand. Nevertheless such scenes, and others like them, can be regarded with amused affection: they all add to the sweetness and merriment of life. Everything to do with the divine must be inclusive. It is interesting to note how all-embracing is the vocabulary of humour.

What is like Jove is *jovial*. Language connects wit with spiritual profundity. The ancestry of the word *wit* links it with understanding and knowledge and thus the knowledge that may delight some clerical don. The German *witz* means both joke and acumen. The French word *spirituel* may mean either witty or spiritually profound. To *amuse* comes from muse. The words genial and genius are related. *Ludicrous* comes from a Latin word for play and thus the play of clerical athletes. *Comic* comes from a Greek word describing a village revel, a form of which was the Church Ale – described on p. 143. *Jest* has roots in the Old French for a noble deed.

Three figures will serve to elucidate wit a little further, to offer a taste of wit and to show how it works: Sydney Smith, Richard Whately and William Temple. Their short sayings in this opening chapter reveal the soul of wit better than lengthy attempts to explain it. Such attempts inevitably end up by being ponderous so that the explainers themselves become a joke, forgetting Shakespeare's wisdom in *Hamlet*: 'Brevity is the soul of wit.'

I   *Masters of the Art*

POOR BUT MERRY: SYDNEY SMITH

The Reverend Canon Sydney Smith (1771–1845) was, in an age of wits, known as both the Smith of Smiths and the Wit of Wits.[1] Educated at Winchester, he became a Fellow of New College, Oxford. He first revealed his wit as Editor of *The Edinburgh Review*, of which he was one of the founders. He became a country parson at Foston-le-Clay in Yorkshire. Here for twenty years he faithfully ministered to a flock of some three hundred souls, before moving to the less remote and more attractive living of Combe Florey in Somerset.

In 1831, at the age of fifty-eight, he became a Canon of St Paul's Cathedral. His duties at the cathedral required only three months of official residence every year, and so he did not have to forfeit his country parish and delectable parsonage in Somerset.

He was celebrated for the merriment provoked by his conversation. Mrs Sarah Siddons, the Queen of Tragedy, when she first met him, was determined to preserve her tragic dignity, but after a vain struggle she had violent convulsions of laughter and had to be helped away from the table. Servants, according to Lord Brougham, were occasionally observed leaving the room with tears running down their faces and in peals of unextinguishable laughter.

Lord Byron remarked of him, 'His jokes were sermons and his sermons jokes,' whilst Charles Greville, the celebrated racehorse owner and political diarist, wrote: 'He has the true religion of benevolence and charity, of peace and goodwill to mankind which, let us hope (as I firmly believe) to be all-sufficient, be the truth of the great mystery what it may.'

∾∾∾

Smith was the first to comment: 'She looked as if she had walked straight out of the Ark.'

He also coined the phrase: 'A square peg in a round hole.'

He once saw two women hurling insults at one another across an alleyway in Edinburgh. He turned to his companion and said: 'Those two women will never agree; they are arguing from different premises.'

One evening his friend Mrs Grote entered a drawing room wearing a huge rose-coloured turban. Smith whispered to his companion: 'Now I know the meaning of the word grotesque.'

He said to Mrs Grote: 'Go where you will, do what you please, I have the most perfect confidence in your indiscretion.'

He described the Society for the Suppression of Vice as 'a society for suppressing the vices of persons whose income does not exceed £500 per annum'.

It was impossible for someone of Sydney's originality to rise to high office in his Church. His brother Bobus Smith, by contrast, became Advocate-General of Bengal and later a Member of Parliament. Sydney once said to him: 'You have risen by your gravity; and I have fallen by my levity.'

He said of a friend called Miss Alcock that 'her Latin name should be *Domina Omnis Penis*'.

Someone said of William Whewell, the eminent scientist and philosopher, 'Whewell's forte is science.' 'Yes,' added Smith, 'and his foible is omni-science.'

A pompous man informed Smith that he was compiling a history of distinguished Somersetshire families. Smith said to him: 'I regret not being able to contribute to so valuable a work. We are not a great people at all. We are common honest people – people that pay our bills. We have never had any arms, but have always sealed our letters with our thumbs.'

When he was advised by his doctor to take a daily walk on an empty stomach, he asked: 'Whose?'

∾∾∾

Some sayings of Sydney Smith[2]

Man is certainly a benevolent animal. *A* never sees *B* in distress without thinking that *C* ought to relieve him directly.

Country life is very good: in fact, the best – for cattle.

I have no relish for the country; it is a kind of healthy grave. It is a place with only one post a day … In the country I always fear that creation will expire before tea-time.

What two ideas are more inseparable than Beer and Britannia?

He began to fumble for his brains.

You might as well try to poultice the lump off a camel's back.

∾∾∾

I endeavour in vain to give my parishioners more cheerful ideas of religion; to teach them that God is not a jealous, childish, merciless tyrant; that he is best served by a regular tenor of good actions, – not by bad singing, ill-composed prayers, and eternal apprehensions. But the luxury of false religion is, to be unhappy.

∾∾∾

There is no more interesting spectacle than to see the effects of wit upon the different characters of men; than to observe it expanding caution, relaxing dignity, unfreezing coldness – teaching age, and care, and pain, to smile, – extorting reluctant gleams of pleasure from melancholy, and charming even the pangs of grief. It is pleasant to observe how it

penetrates through the coldness and awkwardness of society, gradually
bringing men nearer together, and, like the combined force of wine and
oil, giving every man a glad heart and a shining countenance. Genuine
and innocent wit like this, is surely the flavour of the mind.[3]

∾∾∾

When wit is combined with sense and information, when it is soft-
ened by benevolence and restrained by principle, when it is in the
hands of a man who loves humour, justice, decency, good nature,
morality and religion, wit is then a beautiful and delightful part of
our nature. Man could direct his ways by plain reason and support
his life by tasteless food; but God has given us wit and flavour and
brightness and laughter and perfume, to enliven the days of man's
pilgrimage and to charm his pained steps over the burning marl.[4]

∾∾∾

I thank God who has made me poor that he has made me merry.

WIT WITH WISDOM: RICHARD WHATELY

Sydney Smith's near contemporary Richard Whately (1787–1863) was
educated at Oriel College, Oxford. He became Fellow of Oriel in
1811, Rector of Halesworth in East Suffolk in 1822, Principal of
St Alban Hall, Oxford, in 1825, and Drummond Professor of Political
Economy in 1829.

In 1831 he became the Anglican Archbishop of Dublin. There he
was actively involved in the political and religious life of Ireland,
especially in his work as a Commissioner of National Education.

∾∾∾

Some of Archbishop Whately's remarks are good examples of wisdom couched with wit:

Honesty is the best policy; but he who is governed by that policy is not an honest man.

Everyone wishes to have truth on his side, but it is not everyone that sincerely wishes to be on the side of truth.

It is folly to expect men to do all that they may reasonably be expected to do.

Preach not because you have to say something, but because you have something to say.

Happiness is no laughing matter.

∾∾∾

As Archbishop, Whately got on well with the young men about the Viceregal Court in Dublin. One of them, who was aide-de-camp to the Lord-Lieutenant, mistakenly supposed that the archbishop was hostile towards Roman Catholic bishops.

'My Lord Archbishop,' said the aide-de-camp, 'do you know what is the difference between a Roman Catholic bishop and a donkey?'

'No,' said the archbishop.

'The one has a cross on his breast and the other on his back,' replied the aide-de-camp.

'Ha,' said the archbishop, 'do you know the difference between an aide-de-camp and a donkey?'

'No,' said the aide-de-camp.

'Neither do I,' answered the archbishop.

∾∾∾

When asked to compare two great speakers, Whately is reputed to have said:

When the moon shines brightly we say, 'How beautiful the moon is'; and when the sun shines we say, 'How beautiful the field, the trees and hills.' Of the sun itself we do not speak. So the best orator is like the sun – you think only of the thing he advocates. The second best is like the moon – you think only of him.

THE SOUL OF WIT: WILLIAM TEMPLE

William Temple (1881–1944) was a greatly gifted Archbishop of Canterbury, but only occupied the see for two and a half years before his untimely death on 26 October 1944. He was the second son of Frederick Temple, another Archbishop of Canterbury. Amongst his appointments were Fellow of Queen's College, Oxford, in 1904, Headmaster of Repton in 1910, Rector of St James's Piccadilly in 1914, Bishop of Manchester in 1921, and Archbishop of York in 1929. There have been many studies of his religious philosophy and social concerns.

William Temple was another figure who exemplified the soul of wit. It was said that it was impossible to give an adequate impression of him to anyone who had never seen him nor felt the exhilaration of his company, nor heard his enormous Homeric laughter. His official biographer, F. A. Iremonger, ended his book[5] with the comment of a Cumberland shepherd: 'He was a very jolly man.' Alan Watts claimed that Temple had a belly-laugh which could be heard for miles. He wrote: 'It rang out like church bells bewitched by elves. It undulated in the air so as to make weak leaves fall from the trees. There never was such a laugh in Christendom.'[6]

∾∾∾

When he was a young pupil at Rugby a master was discussing one of his essays with him and asked: 'Are you not a little bit out of your depth here?' The confident schoolboy answered: 'Perhaps, Sir, but I can swim.'

His explanation of how he put up with bores at diocesan conferences was: 'By prolonged bouts of inattention.'

He was once asked: 'My aunt was suddenly prevented from going on a ship that went down – would you call that a case of providential interference?' He replied: 'Can't tell; didn't know your aunt.'

A youthful critic once said to him: 'You only believe what you believe because your parents conditioned you.' Temple responded: 'And you only believe that I believe what I believe because my parents conditioned me because your parents conditioned you.'

∾∾∾

Remarks attributed to William Temple

It is not the ape, nor the tiger in man that I fear, but the donkey.

I believe in the Church, One Holy, Catholic and Apostolic, and I regret that it nowhere exists.

It is a mistake to suppose that God is only, or even chiefly, concerned with religion.

About the Church

THE CHURCH MADE VISIBLE

The Church is made visible by its buildings. Churches have an outside, a churchyard; and they have an inside, often largely occupied by pews. One man, Sir Christopher Wren, who lived between 1632 and 1723, graced an entire city with his church architecture, where landmark after landmark is his work.

The Church is also visible in its gatherings, in the church-going of its members. The humour in this is in the disparity between sincere worship and attendance for curiosity or ostentation.

It could be claimed that what is vital about the Church is invisible. It is the hidden and unsung acts of charity by Christians. There are also unseen characteristic traits about certain denominations of the Church and religious orders. These can give rise to humour and are exemplified by the Church of England.

THE OUTSIDE: THE CHURCHYARD

Beneath those rugged elms, that yew-tree's shade,
Where heaves the turf in many a mouldering heap,
Each in his narrow cell for ever laid,
The rude forefathers of the hamlet sleep.

Thomas Gray, *Elegy Written in a Country Churchyard*

Churchyard maintenance is becoming increasingly difficult, and it will be appreciated if parishioners will cut the
grass round their own graves.

> A note from a parish priest in his monthly paper

∾∾∾

R.I.P.

A girl in our village makes love in the churchyard.
She doesn't care who, but it must be the churchyard.
They say she prefers the old part to the new.
Green granite chippings, maybe,
Rankle. Worn slabs welcome.
And after, in her bedroom,
She sees the mirror's view
Of her shoulder embossed
In Loving Memory.
Ann, why do you do it, you've eight O-levels?
Why not, Ann? If bones remember, you'll give them joy.
It's as good a place as any,
Close by nave, rood screen, chapel of ease,
Peal of the bells,
Bob Singles and Grandsire Doubles,
And when you half close your eyes,
The horned gargoyles choose.
But it has to happen.
Oh, Ann, tonight you were levelled.
William Jones, late of this parish,
Was cold beneath you, and his great-great grandson
Warm above; and you rose,
Though your shoulder didn't know it,
In Glorious Expectation of the Life to Come.

Alan Garner[1]

THE INSIDE: THE PEWS

There have been smiles created around various parts of a church: by the font with the christenings; at the organ and choir stalls with the music; in the pulpit with the sermons; and on epitaphs, both inside and outside the building.

'Pew' is a modern spelling of 'pue'. The word comes from 'pui', the Old French for a 'raised place'. In the seventeenth century 'horse-box pews' became fashionable and the wealthy equipped their own pew with every comfort. Two verses made fun of this sort of seating.

> O my own darling pue, which might serve for a bed,
> With its cushions so soft and its curtains of red;
> Of my half waking visions that pue is the theme,
> And when sleep seals my eyes, of my pue still I dream.
>> John Noake, *The Rambler in Worcestershire*, 1851

> A bedstead of the antique mode,
> Compact of timber many a load,
> Such as our ancestors did use,
> Was metamorphosed into pews;
> Which still their ancient nature keep
> By lodging folk disposed to sleep.
>> Jonathan Swift, *Baucis and Philemon*[2]

CHRISTOPHER WREN

Christopher Wren was an inventor, mathematician, astronomer, draughtsman, and eventually England's most famous architect. Nevertheless, even such a description hardly does justice to all his manifold abilities. He lived for ninety years and through the reigns of seven kings and queens. After the Great Fire of London in 1666, he drew up plans for a new City of London, but they were turned

down. Instead, he built the new St Paul's Cathedral and supervised
the building of it, as well as building or rebuilding over fifty other
churches, all different from each other.

He was buried in the great cathedral he designed. His epitaph
in Latin, written by his son, reads: *Si monumentum requiris, circum-
spice* – If you seek a monument, look around you. This refers to
St Paul's, of course, but it might also equally apply to the City
of London itself. Perhaps no other individual has ever stamped a
city so vividly and visually with the presence of the Christian
Church.

Four amusing verses celebrate his achievements, and one charming letter indicates his own wit.

> I've always considered Sir Christopher Wren,
> As an architect, one of the greatest of men;
> And, talking of Epitaphs – much I admire his,
> 'Circumspice, si Monumentum requiris',
> Which an erudite Verger translated to me,
> 'If you ask for his Monument, Sir-come-spy-see!'
>
> Richard Harris Barnum, *The Cynotaph*

> Clever men
> Like Christopher Wren
> Only occur just now and then.
> No one expects
> In perpetuity
> Architects of his ingenuity;
> No, never a cleverer dipped his pen
> Than clever Sir Christopher – Christopher Wren,
> With his chaste designs
> On classical lines,
> His elegant curves and neat inclines.
> For all day long he'd measure and limn
> Till the ink gave out or the light grew dim,
> And if a Plan
> Seemed rather baroque or too 'Queen Anne'
> (As Plans well may),

He'd take a look
At his pattern book
And do it again in a different way.
Every day of the week was filled
With a church to mend or a church to build,
And never an hour went by but when
London needed Sir Christopher Wren.
'Bride's in Fleet Street lacks a spire.
Mary-le-Bow a nave and choir.'
'Please to send the plans complete
For a new Saint Stephen's, Coleman Street.'
'Pewterer's Hall is much too tall,
Kindly lower the N.W. wall.'
'Salisbury Square,
Decidedly bare
Can you put one of your churches there?'
'Dome of St. Paul's is not yet done,
Dean's been waiting since half-past one.'
London calling
From ten till ten,
London calling
Christopher Wren!

                                        Hugh Chesterman[3]

Sir Christopher Wren came to the field of fire,
And graced it with spire,
And nave and choir,
Careful column and carven tier;
That the ships coming up from the sea
Should hail where the Wards of Ludgate fall,
A coronel cluster of steeples tall,
All Hallows, Barking by the Wall,
St. Bride, St. Swithin,
St. Catherine Coleman,
St. Margaret Pattens,
St. Mary-le-Bow,
St. Nicholas Cole Abbey,

St. Alban, Wood Street,
St. Magnus the Martyr,
St. Edmond the King
Whose names like a chime so sweetly call,
And high over all
The Cross and Ball,
On the Riding Redoubtable Dome of St. Paul.

Sir John Squire[4]

Sir Christopher Wren
Said, 'I am going to dine with some men,
If anyone calls
Say I'm designing St. Paul's.'

E. C. Bentley[5]

The Watch

The bride-to-be of Christopher Wren, Faith, daughter of Sir John Coghill of Bletchington, Oxford, dropped a watch in water and asked him to repair it. He returned it with this note:

Madam, The artificer having never before mett with a drowned Watch, like an ignorant physician has been soe long about the cure that he hath made me very unquiet that your commands should be soe long deferred; however, I have sent the watch at last and envie the felicity of it, that it should be so neer your side, and soe often enjoy your Eye, and be consulted by you how your Time shall passe while you employ your hand in your excellent workes. But have a care of it, or I put such a Spell upon it that every Beating of the Balance will tell you 'tis the pulse of my Heart which labours as much to serve you and more Trewly than the watch; for the watch I believe will sometimes lie, and sometimes perhaps be idle and unwilling to goe, having received so much injury by being drenched in that briny bath, that I dispair it should ever be a Trew Servant to you more. But as for me (unless you

drown me too in my Teares) you may be confident I shall
never cease to be,

> Your most affectionate, humble servant,
>
> Chr. Wren

CHURCH-GOING

Perhaps the most lasting pleasure of life is the pleasure of
NOT going to church.   Dean R. W. Inge

> Some go to church to see the Squire,
> Some go his daughter to admire,
> Some go to wink and some to nod,
> But very few to worship God.
>
> Anon.

There are not wanting indications that many come to all
our churches who would not be found there, were they
less influenced by the respectabilities; that many are there
rather from habit and regard for appearances, rather than
from real respect for Christ's ordinance of social worship
and real desire for Christian edification.

A. Mackennel, a Congregational minister, 1967

> Some folk to the church repair
> Not for the preaching
> But for the music there.
>
> Anon.

It used to be said of the first Earl of Eldon, that, notwithstanding his strong religious opinions, he went rarely to
Divine worship, and was 'rather a buttress than a pillar of
the Church, for he supported it only from without'.

Sir Bernard Burke

Many come to bring their clothes to church rather than
themselves.   Anon.

Lavinia is polite, but not profane;
To church as constant as to Drury Lane.
She decently, in form, pays heaven its due;
And makes a civil visit to her pew.
Her lifted fan, to give a solemn air,
Conceals her face, which passes for a prayer:
Curtsies to courtiers, then, with grace, succeed;
Not one the fair omits, but at the creed.
Or if she joins the service, 'tis to speak;
Through dreadful silence the pent heart might break;
Untaught to bear it, women talk away
To God himself, and fondly think they pray.
But sweet their accent, and their air refined;
For they're before their Maker – and mankind:
When ladies once are proud of praying well,
Satan himself will toll the parish bell.

                                              Edward Young

A Complaint

To see a strange and outlandish fowl,
A quaint baboon, an ape, an owl,
A dancing bear, a giant's bone,
A foolish engine move alone,
A morris-dance, a puppet play,
Mad Tom to sing a roundelay,
A woman dancing on a rope,
Bull-baiting also at the Hope,
A rimer's jests, a juggler's cheats,
A tumbler showing cunning feats,
Or players acting on the stage, –
There goes the bounty of our age!
But unto any pious motion
There's little coin and less devotion.

                                              Henry Farley

On St. Paul's

This is God's House, but 'tis to be deplor'd
More come to see the House than serve the Lord.

Anon.

Whenever God erects a house of prayer,
The Devil always builds a chapel there;
And 'twill be found, upon examination,
The latter has the largest congregation.

Daniel Defoe

No rain nor snow can make us stay
    If we have tickets for the play;
But let one drop the walk besmirch,
    And it's too wet to go to church.

Anon.

∾∾∾

The Archbishop of York invited Lord Melbourne to the evening service. The archbishop was disconcerted by Melbourne's response: 'No, my Lord, once is orthodox, twice is puritanical.'

∾∾∾

Church-going

Once I am sure there's nothing going on
I step inside, letting the door thud shut.
Another church: matting, seats, and stone,
And little books; sprawlings of flowers, cut
For Sunday, brownish now; some brass and stuff
Up at the holy end; the small neat organ;
And a tense, musty, unignorable silence,
Brewed God knows how long. Hatless, I take off
My cycle-clips in awkward reverence,

Move forward, run my hand around the font.
Form where I stand, the roof looks almost new –
Cleaned or restored? Someone would know: I don't.
Mounting the lectern, I peruse a few
Hectoring large-scale verses, and pronounce
'Here endeth' much more loudly than I'd meant.
The echoes snigger briefly. Back at the door
I sign the book, donate an Irish sixpence,
Reflect the place was not worth stopping for.

Yet stop I did: in fact I often do,
And always end much at a loss like this,
Wondering what to look for; wondering, too,
When churches fall completely out of use
What we shall turn them into, if we shall keep
A few cathedrals chronically on show,
Their parchment, plate and pyx* in locked cases,
And let the rest rent-free to rain and sheep.
Shall we avoid them as unlucky places?

Or, after dark, will dubious women come
To make their children touch a particular stone;
Pick simples† for a cancer; or on some
Advised night see walking a dead one?
Power of some sort or other will go on
In games, in riddles, seemingly at random;
But superstition, like belief, must die,
And what remains when disbelief has gone?
Grass, weedy pavement, brambles, buttress, sky,

A shape less recognizable each week,
A purpose more obscure. I wonder who
Will be the last, the very last, to seek
This place for what it was; one of the crew

---

* *Pyx:* box used in the Roman Catholic church to hold the bread or wafer (the 'host') after it has been consecrated
† *Simples:* medicinal herbs

That tap and jot and know what rood-lofts* were?
Some ruin-bibber, randy for antique,
Or Christmas-addict, counting on a whiff
Of gown-and-bands and organ-pipes and myrrh?
Or will he be my representative,

Bored, uninformed, knowing the ghostly silt†
Dispersed, yet tending to this cross of ground
Through suburb scrub because it held unspilt
So long and equably what since is found
Only in separation – marriage, birth,
And death, and thoughts of these – for which was built
This special shell? For, though I've no idea
What this accoutred frowsty barn is worth,
It pleases me to stand in silence here;

A serious house on serious earth it is,
In whose blent air all our compulsions meet,
Are recognized, and robed as destinies.
And that much never can be obsolete,
Since someone will forever be surprising
A hunger in himself to be more serious,
And gravitating with it to this ground,
Which, he once heard, was proper to grow wise in,
If only that so many dead lie round.

                                    Philip Larkin[6]

THE CHURCH OF ENGLAND

Faithful sons and daughters of the Church of England have much to
love: the architecture of cathedral and parish churches; the beauty of
the liturgy of *The Book of Common Prayer* and the King James transla-

---

* *Rood-loft:* a gallery over the ornamental partition separating the nave from the
  chancel
† *Silt:* fine sediment

tion of the Bible; the poetic and comic genius of some priests; the distinctive choral heritage; the formidable scholarship of certain divines; the comprehensiveness and tolerance. Often they find themselves loving precisely those things about which hostile critics complain.

Who else but an Anglican cleric could refer to 'the truly extraordinary behaviour of Judas Iscariot'? Who else but a native son of the established Church could say in a Christmas Day sermon, as one Dean of Christ Church did, 'Nor can I do better, in conclusion, than to impress upon you the importance of the study of Greek literature, which not only elevates above the common herd, but leads not infrequently to positions of considerable emolument'?

∾∾∾

When I mention religion, I mean the Christian religion, and not only the Christian religion, but the Protestant religion; and not only the Protestant religion, but the Church of England.

Parson Thwackum in *Tom Jones* by Henry Fielding

A young emigrant girl wrote the following letter to Lady Laura Ridding, the wife of the then Bishop of Southwell:

Dear Madam, I hope this finds you as it leaves me. This ship is in the middle of the Red Sea. and it is fearfully hot. I am in a terrible state of melting all day long. But honoured Madam, I know that you will be pleased to hear that I am still a member of the Church of England.

Roman Catholics claim to be infallible; Anglicans to be always right.   Richard Steele

The merit claimed for the Anglican Church is, that if you let it alone, it will let you alone.   Ralph Waldo Emerson

3   *At Momentous Moments*

BAPTISMS

... when I got to the Chapel my beard moustache and whiskers were so stiff with ice that I could hardly open my mouth and my beard was frozen on to my mackintosh. There was a large christening party from Llwyn Gwilym. The baby was baptised in ice which was broken and swimming about in the Font.

Francis Kilvert, diary entry for 13 February, 1870[1]

Then the Vicar of Fordington told us of the state of things in his parish when he first came to it nearly half a century ago. No man had ever been known to receive the Holy Communion except the parson, the clerk and the sexton. There were 16 women communicants and most of them went away when he refused to pay them for coming. They had been accustomed there at some place in the neighbourhood to pass the cup to each other with a nod of the head. At one church there were two male communicants. When the cup was given to the first he touched his forelock and said, 'Here's your good health, sir.' The other said, 'Here's the good health of our Lord Jesus Christ.'

One day there was Christening and no water in the Font. 'Water, Sir!' said the clerk in astonishment, 'The last parson never used no water. He spit into his hand.'

Ibid., April 1874

Parson Hawker of Morwenstow baptized with gusto. He would raise the child high in his arms, carry it down the church, and thunder out: 'We receive this child into the congregation of Christ's Flock.'

Robert Stephen Hawker (1804–75) was a famously eccentric Cornish clergyman whose first biography, by Sabine Baring-Gould, was published only a year after his death.[2] A more recent biographer wrote of him that there was a battle within him 'between pride, vanity, dogmatism, irascibility, malice, superstition and courage, charitableness, humour, affection, humaneness, piety'.[3]

∾∾∾

Parson John Skelton of Diss in Norfolk also held children aloft at baptisms – including some that he himself had proudly fathered by his own mistress. In Skelton's day it was still illegal for the clergy to marry. He lived from around 1460 to 1529 and had been tutor to Prince Henry (later King Henry VIII) before holding the living of Diss for twenty-five years. He is generally considered to have been the first poet laureate, and was buried in Westminster Abbey.

∾∾∾

Sabine Baring-Gould (1834–1924), Hawker's biographer, was a squire-parson and prolific author, best remembered nowadays for his hymn, 'Onward, Christian soldiers'. One of his anecdotes concerns an old scholar-parson who, at the private christenings of the children of one of the labourers in his parish, was always provided with a bottle of rum, a pack of cards, a lemon, and a basin of pure water. The rector would return to the rectory very late and very inebriated. The housekeeper left only the library window open for him. Beneath it was a bed of violets, and there, when he was unable to heave himself to the sill, he often 'slept off his exertion'.

∾∾∾

The babe, with a cry brief and dismal,
Fell into the water baptismal;
Ere they'd gathered its plight,
It had sunk out of sight,
For the depth of the font was abysmal.

Anon.

When I was christened
They held me up
and poured some water
out of a cup.

The trouble was
it fell on me
and I and water
don't agree.

A lot of christeners
stood and listened:
I let them know
that I was christened.

David McCord[4]

At many baptisms the paternity of the child has been the subject of lively speculation. A newspaper report of a christening in 1980 mentioned that the proud and happy mother was flanked by six handsome young men. She was the somewhat wayward daughter of a peer. Any of the six might have been the father. She did not know which one. Each man was a godfather and each godfather contributed one name to the baby's forename. For his surname he was given his mother's maiden name.

❧❧❧

Other ladies were more modest about the paternity of their offspring. One wife, for example, made a brave attempt to preserve her reputation at her child's christening at St Dunstan's Church, Stepney, on 4 August 1641. The baptismal entry reads:

Gabrielle son of Anstis the wife of Thomas Preston of Ratcliff Highway, mariner, whom she affirmeth to be begotten by her said husband who is yet reported to have been forth at sea ever since midsummer, A.D. 1640, 4 days old.

Fine day. I baptised Sarah, the Bastard Daughter of the Widow Smallwood of Eaton, aged near 50, whose husband died above a year ago.

William Cole, diary entry for 3 March, 1766[5]

Baptism: Thomas William the illegitimate Son of Maria Haws and the Soldiers of Kew Barracks.

Entry in the Baptism Register of
Chiswick Parish Church, 1 July, 1798

There have been several very curious entries in parish baptism registers. One from Purleigh in Essex reflected the custom of buying and selling wives, sometimes by auction. It recorded the baptism of Amie, the daughter of Moses Stebbing 'by a bought Wife delivered to him by a Halter, Sep 1782'.

There were two other strange entries from the baptism register of Winchcombe in Gloucestershire. The first was dated 1569: 'John, son of an adventure at Oliver Mackrell's'.

The second was dated 1747 and recorded the baptism of the illegitimate Cunosua Almsbury. The entry noted: 'This child was exposed and preserved by dogs which defended it from the swine.' This probably explains the name, no doubt given by the priest. 'Cuno' suggests the Greek word for a dog.

∾∾∾

There was a sad mishap at the baptism of the infant daughter of the Duke and Duchess of Chandos by a nineteenth-century Archbishop of Canterbury. The Archbishop casually remarked that he had 'never christened a more quiet child'. It was not surprising. The baby was in fact dead – 'expired under a load of lace'.

∾∾∾

A Norfolk clergyman refused to christen a certain Mr Tuck's son Uz. Together with Og it is the shortest name in the Bible. The frustrated father then insisted that his son should have the longest name: Mahershalalashbaz.

CONFIRMATIONS

At a confirmation an individual has the opportunity to make the promises made for him or her at baptism his own. A bishop conducts the ceremony and lays hands on the heads of the candidates. Episcopal behaviour on these occasions can be odd.

∾∾∾

St Hugh was the much-loved Bishop of Lincoln in the twelfth century. It was a huge diocese and there were often so many candidates at his confirmations that he conducted them on horseback.

∾∾∾

Of Richard Corbet, who was made Bishop of Oxford in 1628 and Bishop of Norwich in 1632, John Aubrey wrote:

> One time, as he was confirming, the country people pressing in to see the ceremonie, sayd he, 'beare-off there, or I'le confirme yee with my staffe.' Another time being to lay his hand on the head of a man very bald, he turns to his chaplaine (Lushington) and sayd 'Some dust, Lushington', (to keep his hand from slipping). There was a

man with a great venerable beard; sayd the bishop, 'You, behind the beard'.[6]

∾∾∾

The nonconformist divine Richard Baxter (1615–91) left nearly two hundred works of deep spirituality which reflect his love of moderation. He wrote several hymns, including 'Ye holy angels bright' and 'He wants not friends who hath Thy love'. Baxter had once been offered the Bishopric of Hereford, but declined it because he was dissatisfied with the current Anglican view of episcopacy; from the passage below, his disillusionment with the established Church seems quite understandable.

When I was a schoolboy about fifteen years of age, the Bishop coming into the country, many went to be confirmed. We that were boys ran out to see the Bishop among the rest, not knowing anything of the meaning of the business. When we came thither, we met about thirty or forty in all, of our own stature and temper, that had come for us to be 'bishopped', as then it was called. The Bishop examined us not at all in one article of the Faith; but in a churchyard in haste we were set in rank, and he passed hastily over us, laying his hands on our head, and saying a few words, which neither I nor any that I spoke with, understood; so hastily were they uttered and a very short prayer recited, and there was an end. But whether we were Christians or infidels, or knew as much as that there was a God, the Bishop little knew or inquired. And yet he was esteemed one of the best Bishops in England. And though the Canons require that the curate or minister send a certificate that children have learned the Catechism, yet there was no such thing done, but we ran of our own accord to see the Bishop only; and almost all the rest of this country had not this much. This was the old careless practice of this excellent duty of Confirmation.[7]

Francis Kilvert recorded in his diary that there was a time when a
young clergyman arrived late with his candidate at a confirmation
and the domineering bishop rebuked them for being late, made
them both kneel down, and confirmed them both!

ತುಲ∾ುಲ

Confirmation at Eton: Like a huge garden party, faintly
overshadowed by a sense of religion.   A. C. Benson

ತುಲ∾ುಲ

'Princess Vicky', Queen Victoria's eldest daughter, was confirmed
in the chapel at Windsor Castle in 1856. She was dressed in what
The Times described as a 'rich silk lace gown, with five flounces
pinked, the body richly trimmed with white riband and Mechlin
lace'. Lord Granville, the leader of the Liberals in the House of
Lords, commented acidly: 'The Princess Royal went through her
part well. The Princess Alice cried violently. The Archbishop read
what seemed a dull address; luckily it was inaudible. The Bishop of
Oxford rolled out a short prayer with conscious superiority.'

WEDDINGS

Many people were amused in the film *Four Weddings and a Funeral*
at the bumbling verbal errors of the vicar during one of the marriage
services. Perhaps the most comical mistake, not used in the film, is
one that has been often reported. It occurs when the clergyman asks
if any impediment is known why a couple may not be lawfully
joined in Holy Matrimony. The spoonerism is to say 'joyfully loined'
together. The very error could be regarded as a pleasing improve-
ment to the traditional Anglican order of service. (For more on
spoonerisms, see p. 133–4.)

ತುಲ∾ುಲ

When the biblical scholar Julius Hare gave a charge to the clergy and archdeaconry of Lewes in 1841 he reported that in his own parish of Hurstmonceux – and in others too, so he had heard – numbers of brides among the lower orders were wont to come to be married 'with the offspring of unhallowed lust lying beneath their bosoms'!

∾∾∾

An anecdote is told of a vicar who said to the kneeling couple at the chancel steps: 'Follow me.' He proceeded to the altar, but was puzzled to hear an odd shuffling noise behind him. When he turned round he saw that they had followed him to the altar rail on their knees.

∾∾∾

Joshua Brooke was a vicar in Manchester in the mid-nineteenth century. It was his custom to line up a dozen or more couples and marry them at one time. This system fell apart in his old age when he married a wrong couple. The couple, however, took an instant fancy to each other. They rejected offers of Nullification by Special Decree, the passionate pleas of their intended spouses, and various threats from their families, and fled to Blackpool.

∾∾∾

In the eighteenth century marriages were legal even if conducted outside churches. No banns, ring, witnesses, licence or registration were required. Conducting them became a lucrative trade. Defrocked or sham clergymen would marry for a fee any couple who came to them with no questions asked. The taverns near the Fleet prison in London became notorious for these transactions.

Jonathan Swift (on whom see p. 95) is believed to have conducted such a casual wedding while on one of his journeys between London and Chester, and to have written this rhyming marriage certificate:

Under an oak in stormy weather,
I joined this rogue and whore together;
And none but he who rules the thunder
Can part this whore and rogue asunder.

∽∽∽

Two aldermen, three lawyers, five physicians
Seven captains, with nine poets, ten musicians,
Woo'd all one wench. She, weighing all conditions
By which she might attain to most promotion,
Did take a priest at last for pure devotion.

Sir John Harington[8]

∽∽∽

Marriage resembles a pair of shears, so joined that they
cannot be separated, often moving in opposite directions,
yet always punishing anyone who comes between them.

Sydney Smith[9]

∽∽∽

I married Tom Burge of Ansford to Charity Andrews of
C. Cary by Licence this morning. The Parish of Cary made
him marry her, and he came handbolted to Church for
fear of running away . . .

James Woodforde, diary entry for 22 November, 1768[10]

Like Francis Kilvert (see p. 20), Parson Woodforde (1740–1803) was
a notable clergyman diarist. Although he lived in obscurity and
tranquillity he recorded some domestic or parochial detail almost
every day after he started keeping his diary in 1758.

FUNERALS

The novelist Henry James is said to have told a story of two clergy-men asked by mistake to conduct the same funeral. One came first and got no further than 'I am the Resurrection and the Life', when the other entered. '*I* am the Resurrection and the Life,' cried the latter.

∽∽∽

The doctor and the parson were standing by the bed of an old man as he lay dying.
  'I'm afraid he's gone,' said the priest.
  'Yes, he has,' said the doctor.
  'No, I baint,' murmured the patient, feebly sitting up.
  'Lie down, dear,' said his wife, 'doctor and parson know best.'

∽∽∽

Father Healy of Bray was an Irish Roman Catholic priest celebrated for his wit. As he lay dying an old friend of his was also sinking fast. When this news was brought to him he said: 'I'm afraid then that it is going to be a dead heat.'

∽∽∽

When a Reverend Mr Ellerbeck conducted the funeral of the first Earl of Lowther, it was claimed that the ghost of the deceased earl rudely and abruptly pushed the clergyman out of his pulpit during the ceremony.

∽∽∽

In the reign of Charles II there was a famous lady of easy virtue called Madam Creswell. She died in prison. In her will she left £10 for the preacher of her funeral sermon on the condition that he only spoke well of her. After talking about morality in general, the preacher finished with these words:

> By the will of the deceased, it is expected that I should mention her, and say nothing but what was well of her. All that I shall say of her, therefore, is this: She was born well, she lived well, and she died well; for she was born with the name of Creswell, she lived in Clerkenwell, and she died in Bridewell.

∾∾∾

> Her funeral sermon (which was long
> And followed by a sacred song)
> Mentioned her virtues it is true
> But dwelt upon her vices too.
>
> Hilaire Belloc[11]

∾∾∾

The generally saintly and warm-hearted Theodoret (*c.*393–*c.*466) obviously suffered a lapse of character when writing a letter, dated 444, on the death of Archbishop Cyril of Alexandria, with whom he had long been engaged in theological controversy:

> At last with a final struggle, the villain has passed away. Observing that his malice increased daily and injured the body of the Church, the Governor of our souls has lopped him off like a cancer. His departure delights the survivors, but possibly disheartens the dead; there is some fear that under the provocation of his company they may send him back again to us. Care must therefore be taken to order the Guild of Undertakers to place a very big and heavy stone on his grave to stop him coming back here. I am glad and rejoice to see the fellowship of the Church delivered from such a contagion; but I am sad and sorry

as I reflect that the wretched man never took rest from his misdeeds, and died designing greater and worse.[12]

∾∾∾

In his last will and testament, a cynical bishop left this verse:

> Tell my priests, when I am gone,
> O'er me to shed no tears,
> For I shall be no deader then
> Than they have been for years.
> > Anon.

The Hearse Verse

The Old Grey Hearse goes rolling by,
You don't know whether to laugh or cry;
For you know some day it'll get you too,
And the hearse's next load may consist of you.

They'll take you out, and they'll lower you down,
While men with shovels stand all around;
They'll throw in dirt, and they'll throw in rocks,
And they won't give a damn if they break the box.

And your eyes drop out and your teeth fall in,
And the worms crawl over your mouth and chin;
They invite their friends and their friends' friends too,
And you look like hell when they're through with you.

> Anon.

4   *At Divine Services*

SUNDAYS

Sundays are the chief days for church services, and once it was frequently thought that attending these services was the only proper activity for a Sunday. The rigidity of attitude about this became a joke itself; and wits were not slow to expose the hypocrisy sometimes associated with this attitude. The Lord's Day Observance Society in particular became a target for derision. It is easy to see why. A reporter once asked an official of the society to comment on a new campaign about Sunday observance. He said: 'We do not give statements on Sunday.'

> We shelled the Turks from 9 to 11 then, being Sunday, had Divine Service.   Royal Navy Commander to the Admiralty, 1915

> As I was going to shave myself this morning as usual on Sundays, my razor broke in my hand as I was setting it on the strop without any violence. May it be always a warning to me not to shave on the Lord's Day or do any other work to profane it pro futuro.
>   James Woodforde, diary entry for 12 March, 1769[1]

> I am always pleased with the hilarity which reigns everywhere in France on this day, and thought it perhaps more conformable to the intention with which a periodical resting from labour was ordained than the mournful and sombre manner in which the day is passed in England.
>   Anne Plumtree, a visitor to France in 1810

Golf may be played on Sunday, not being a game within
the view of the law, but being a form of moral effort.

Stephen Leacock

∽∿∽

Sunday Shopping

When all the other shops are closed on Sunday, the
wretched little sweet stuff shops maintain full trade with
unblushing effrontery. In the windows are displayed vari-
egated sugarsticks, hardbake, toffy, tomtrot, drops, bulls-
eyes and all the rest of the sweet stuff tribe which are dear
to children – no wonder that on a Sunday afternoon one
sees a crowd of the little creatures five or six deep round
the open doors and brilliant windows of these pernicious
places. from a letter to *Church Times*, 1864

∽∿∽

Cheap excursion trains were first introduced in the middle of the
nineteenth century. According to an old school history book, the
then Vice-Chancellor of the University of Cambridge strongly dis-
approved. He wrote as follows to the railway company concerned:

The Vice-Chancellor of the University of Cambridge presents his compliments to the Directors of the Eastern
Counties Railway and begs to inform them that he has
learnt with regret that it is the intention of the Directors
of the Eastern Counties Railway to run excursion trains to
Cambridge on the Lord's Day, with the object of attracting
foreigners and undesirable characters to the University of
Cambridge on that sacred day. The Vice-Chancellor of the
University of Cambridge wishes to point out to the Directors of the Eastern Counties Railways that such a proceed-
ing would be as displeasing to Almighty God as it is to
the Vice-Chancellor of the University of Cambridge.

The Presbyterian Cat

There was a Presbyterian cat,
Went searching for her prey,
And found a moose within the hoose,
Upon the Sawbath day.

The people were all horrifiet,
And they were grieved sair,
And straightway led that wicked cat
Before the ministaire.

The ministaire was horrifiet,
And unto her did say,
'Oh, naughty cat to catch a moose,
Upon the Sawbath day.'

'The Sawbath's been, fra days of yore,
An institution.'
So they straightway led the wicked cat
To execution.

The higher up the plum tree grows,
The sweeter grow the plums,
The more the cobbler plies his trade,
The broader grow his thumbs.

Anon.

∽∽∽

Victorian and Edwardian writers of improving literature for the young sometimes took a high-handed tone about Sunday observance, forgetful of the many difficulties faced by their working-class readers. In one such book, *Down in a Mine, or, Buried Alive* by George E. Sargent, the young hero (who works down the mine six days a week) successfully resists the 'temptation' to have a lie-in on a Sunday by recalling a verse from a hymn:

This is the day that Christ arose
    So early from the dead;
Why should I then my eyelids close,
    And waste my hours in bed?

This kind of well-meaning but patronizing attitude is cleverly satir-
ized in the following verses:

The Ragged Girl's Sunday

'Oh, dear Mama, that little girl
Forgets this is the day
When children should be clean and neat,
And read, and learn, and pray!

'Her face is dirty and her frock,
Holes in her stockings, see;
Her hair is such a fright, oh dear!
How wicked she must be!

'She's playing in the kennel dirt
With ragged girls and boys;
But *I* would not on Sunday touch
My clean and pretty toys.

'I go to church, and sit so still,
I in the garden walk,
Or take my stool beside the fire,
and hear nice Sunday talk.

'I read my Bible, learn my hymns,
My Cathechism say;
That wicked little girl does not –
She only cares to play!'

                            Mary Bennett

HYMNS

Some hymns are unintentionally funny. There is, for example, something laughable about the blatant complacency of this verse in 'From Greenland's icy mountains' by Reginald Heber (1783–1826), despite the author's eminence as a hymn writer and churchman. He rose to become Bishop of Calcutta and died in India of a stroke while cooling himself off in a swimming pool. His once-famous hymn, which he composed in twenty minutes, has been dropped from all modern hymn books.

> Can we, whose souls are lighted
>> With wisdom from on high,
> Can we to men benighted,
>> The lamp of life deny?

This couplet from an old hymn for the young is similarly self-righteous:

> 'Tis a *credit* to any good girl to be neat,
> But quite a *disgrace* to be fine.

∾∾∾

> I wish to have no wishes left,
> But to leave all to Thee;
> And yet I wish that Thou should'st will
> That which I wish should be.
>> from a hymn by Frederick William Faber

> O may thy powerful word
> Inspire the feeble worm
> To rush into thy kingdom, Lord
> And take it as by storm.
>> from the *Wesleyan Hymn Book*

My soul is like a rusty lock;
Lord, oil it with thy grace;
And rub it, rub it, rub it, Lord,
Until I see Thy face.

from an old Puritan hymn

A story has been told that Thomas Beecham, the owner of the pharmaceutical firm and grandfather of the famous conductor, offered to supply new hymn books to a poor parish in the East End of London. The vicar was grateful for the offer but worried about what Beecham might want in return. Apparently the new books arrived just in time for the Christmas Carol Service and the vicar suddenly realized what the wily man had done. This is what he heard the congregation singing:

Hark, the herald angels sing,
Beecham's pills are just the thing,
For blessed peace and mercy mild,
Two for mother, one for child.

∾∾∾

If I were a cassowary
On the plains of Timbuctoo
I would eat a missionary
Cassock, boots and hymn-book too.

Anon.

Hymn of the Scientific Farmers

We squirt the fields and scatter
Our phosphates on the land:
'Organic waste' and 'humus'
We do not understand.

We slaughter trees in thousands
To sell for what they're worth;
No stems to hold the water,
No roots to bind the earth.

Our farms will turn to deserts
Where not a crop can grow,
But long before that happens
We'll take our gains and go.

We'll strip the lanes of hedges,
No wild-flower must survive,
Nor bird find place to nest in –
Let only insects thrive.

We spray to kill diseases,
And once a cure is made
Some other pest is started;
But that is good for Trade.

We rob the flour of virtue,
We leave a rifled sack;
And then with new synthetics
We almost put it back.

We pump our fowls with hormones
As fast as fast can be;
Consumers die of cancer
But we're not there to see.

Our god is an Equation,
And Profit is our goal:
'Exploit the parts like fury –
Forget about the whole.'

Clive Sansom[2]

Dear Lord and Father of mankind,
Forgive our foolish ways;
For most of us, when asked our mind,
Admit we still most pleasure find
In hymns of ancient days,
In hymns of ancient days.

The simple lyrics, for a start,
Of many a modern song,

Are far too trite to touch the heart;
Enshrine no poetry, no art;
And go on much too long,
And go on much too long.

Patrick Baker[3]

It's Not the Same Any More!

They've brought you up to date, Lord,
Down at St Cecilia's.
They've pensioned off the organ,
And syncopated praise!
What happened to tranquillity?
The silence of eternity
Is hard to hear these days,
Is hard to hear these days.

Send thy deep hush subduing all
Those happy claps that drown
The tender whisper of thy call;
Triumphalism is not all
For sometimes we feel down,
For sometimes we feel down.

Drop thy still dews of quietness
Till all our strummings cease;
Take from our souls the strain and stress
Of always having to be blessed;
Give us a bit of peace,
Give us a bit of peace.

Breathe through the beats of praise-guitar
Thy coolness and thy balm;
Let drum be dumb, bring back the lyre,
Enough of earthquake, wind and fire,
Let's hear it for some calm,
Let's hear it for some calm.

Source unknown

There were three little owls in a wood,
Who sang hymns whenever they could.
What the words were about
One could never make out,
But one felt it was doing them good.

Anon.

MUSIC

There was a large Congregation at Church. Poor old Js.
Smith my clerk made a shocking hand of it in singing this
Afternoon at Church, much laughed at . . .

James Woodforde, diary entry for 1 August, 1791[4]

Dean W. R. Inge of St Paul's confessed that he was a much suffering
unmusical man (his diary abounds with petulant and almost profane
lunges against the dreary and interminable musical services which
he had to attend). Although music may have charms to soothe the
savage breast he did not consider himself to be a savage and on him
it had the opposite effect. He could not pray amidst all the howling
and caterwauling. Here are some of the entries in his diary[5]:

Are we quite sure that the Almighty enjoys being seren-
aded?

They turned the Nicene Creed into an anthem; before the
end I had ceased to believe anything.

'Melodies heard are sweet, but those unheard are sweeter'.
Quite right, John Keats; they are.

If I believed that I shall listen through all eternity to the
seraphim blowing their loud uplifted trumpets, it would
almost deter me from the practice of virtue.

Use not vain repetitions. For ten minutes today the choir
repeated the words 'I wrestle and pray'.

Bishop Samuel Wilberforce (1805–73), the energetic and reforming Bishop of Oxford and later of Winchester, once suggested to a rural clergyman that Gregorian chants were unsuited for a village choir. The rector, erroneously, complained: 'But, my Lord, David sang his psalms to Gregorian melodies.'

'Quite so,' the bishop tartly answered, 'and I don't wonder that Saul cast his javelin at him.'

∾∾∾

It was said that about 1500 Michael Trevella, a chorister at Zennor in Cornwall, charmed a passing mermaid with his tenor voice. She wooed him and won him. The South West Travel Board used to claim that during spring tides he could be heard singing psalms on Sunday evenings during Trinity.

The Choir-boy

And when he sang in choruses
  His voice o'er-topped the rest,
Which is very inartistic,
  But the public liked that best.
Anon.

'An Elephant in Distress . . .'

My first memory ecclesiastical is of a time in which we never saw or heard our vicar . . . Our curate, who lived five miles away, rode over for one dreary service on a Sunday, dined, and we saw him no more during the week. He was much occupied in the pursuit of the fox, which, it is charitable to suppose, he mistook for a wolf, and like a good shepherd was anxious to destroy. The service was literally a duet between the parson and the clerk, except when old John Manners, the bricklayer, gave the keynote for the hymn from his bassoon, a sound which might have been uttered by an elephant in distress, and we sang, or when the curate suddenly emerged from his surplice, which he placed on the side of his reading-pew, and appearing in his academical gown, went up the 'three-decker' to preach. The altar was represented by a small rickety deal table, with a scanty covering of faded and patched green baize, on which were placed the overcoat, hat, and riding-whip of the officiating minister, who made a vestry within the sacrarium, and, sitting there in a huge surplice, had a conversation with the sexton before the service began, and looked as though he were about to have his hair cut.

The font was filled with coffin-ropes, tinder-boxes, and brimstone matches, candle-ends, etc. It was never used for baptisms . . . Sparrows twittered, and bats floated, beneath the rotten timbers of the roof, while beetles and moths, and all manner of flies, found happy homes below. The damp walls represented in fresco 'a green and yellow melancholy', which had a depressing influence upon the spirit, and the darkest and most dismal building of the parish was that called the House of God.

Dean Hole[6]

The Alto's Lament

It's tough to be an alto when you're singing in the
    choir,
The sopranos get the twiddly bits that people all admire,
The basses boom like loud trombones, the tenors shout
    with glee,
But the alto part is on two notes (or, if you're lucky, three).

And when we sing an anthem and we lift our hearts in
    praises
The men get all the juicy bits and telling little phrases.
Of course the trebles sing the tune – they always come
    off best;
The altos only get three notes and twenty-two bars rest.

We practise very hard each week from hymn-book and
    the Psalter,

But when the conductor looks at us our voices start to
    falter;
'Too high! Too low! Too fast! Too slow! You held that
    note too long!'
It doesn't matter what we do – it's certain to be wrong!

Oh! shed a tear for altos, they're the martyrs and they know,
In the ranks of choral singers they're considered very low.
They are so very 'umble that a lot of folk forget 'em;
How they'd love to be sopranos, but their vocal cords
    won't let 'em!

And when the final trumpet sounds and we are wafted
    higher,
Sopranos, basses, tenors – they'll be in the heavenly choir.
While they sing 'Alleluia!' to celestial flats and sharps,
The altos will be occupied with polishing the harps.

'Bob the Organist'

This poem was found behind the vestry door of All Saints' Church,
Four Oaks, Sutton Coldfield.

∾∾∾

This quaint inscription, dated 1585, in Norwich Cathedral, commem-
orates Osberto Parsley, who sang in the choir there for fifty years:

Here lies the Man whose Name in Spight of Death,
Renowned lives by Blast of Golden Fame;
Whose Harmony survives his vital Breath,
Whose Skill no Pride did spot, whose life no Blame,
Whose low estate was blest with quiet Mind;
As our sweet Cords with Discords mixed be;
Whose Life in Seventy and Four Years entwined,
As falleth mellowed Apples from the Tree,
Whose Deeds were Rules, whose Words were Verity;
Who here a Singing-man did spend his Days,
Full Fifty Years in our Church Melody;
His Memory shines bright whom thus we praise.

PRAYERS

Some prayers are splendidly worded and beautifully composed, heart-felt and even heart-rending. King David's weeping prayer, when he heard of the death of his son, is as moving as could be.

> 'O my son Absolom, my son, my son Absolom!
> Would to God that I had died for thee,
> O Absolom, my son, my son!'

Nevertheless, because human beings are often ridiculous creatures our very prayers, like certain hymns, are sometimes unintentionally comic, like the prayer of an old Methodist lay preacher, who said: 'We pray for those who feel old age creeping over them, and other things.'

Some prayers can amuse us simply by their very sturdy realism. Sir Jacob Astley (1579–1652) was a Royalist soldier. This was his concise prayer before the Battle of Edgehill on 23 October, 1642:

> 'Lord! thou knowest how busy I must be this day:
> if I forget thee, do not though forget me.'

The following is a prayer of the Reverend Mr Troutbeck, Chaplain of the Scilly Islands, who evidently had the interests of his flock at heart. It reflects the custom that when ships were wrecked their cargoes were there for the locals to grab.

> 'Dear God, we pray that wrecks shouldn't happen, but if
> it be thy will that they do, we pray Thee let them be for
> the benefit of Thy poor people of Scilly.'

∾∾∾

Adolphus Frederick, Duke of Cambridge, was the seventh son of King George the Third. He was one of Victoria's 'wicked uncles' and was very deaf. He sat at the front of the church during services as fitting his royal status, but this did not mean that he heard everything clearly and he would make loud comments.

When the priest said 'Let us pray', the duke would answer 'Get on with it then.' He responded to a prayer for fine weather by shouting out 'Amen, but you won't get it till the wind drops.'

∾∾∾

In 1837, when praying for the new Queen Victoria, Archbishop Howley got into great confusion. He said, 'King of Queens, Lord of Ladies, the only Ruler of Princesses . . .'

∾∾∾

A guest of the Percys, a large and aristocratic dynasty, attended chapel. He found the place full of Percy pews and Percy memorials. He suggested to the parson that he should begin the service: 'Almighty and most Percyful God . . .'

∾∾∾

A number of odd prayers have their origins in Scotland, like this traditional petition:

> From ghosties and ghoulies
> And long-legged beasties,
> And things that go bump in the night,
> Good Lord, deliver us.

One Scot is said to have prayed: 'O God, grant that I may be right – for Ye ken I never change.'

A Scottish minister prayed for exactly the right sort of wind to get the crops into condition for harvest in these terms: 'O Lord, we pray thee to send us wind, no' a rantin', tantin', tearin', wind, but a noohin', winnin' wind.'

Dean Hole, who was Dean of Rochester and a man of many talents, recorded the prayer of another Scottish minister for Queen Adelaide:

'O Lord, save Thy servant, our sovereign lady the Queen: grant that as she grows an old woman she may become a new man; strengthen her with Thy blessing that she may live a pure virgin, bringing forth sons and daughters to the glory of God; and give her grace that she may go forth before her people like a he-goat on the mountains.'

∾∾∾

Queen Victoria did not put up with any nonsense from her bishops about religion. When one of them said to her, 'Ah, Ma'am, we cannot pray too often or too fervently for the Royal Family,' she answered, 'Not too fervently, no: but too frequently, yes.'

∾∾∾

Often writers deliberately composed humorous prayers. A much-loved and much-quoted poem by John Betjeman was a war-time one entitled 'In Westminster Abbey'. It is a piece of gentle satire about a genteel lady, who thinks only of her own wellbeing, the safety of her home in Cadogan Square and the value of her shares. Having listed her requirements, she hurries off to a luncheon date.

Some comically composed prayers comment on other people. The first is directed against a headstrong young clergyman:

> Thank you, God,
> for our new curate,
> with thy gifts
> so swift to act.
> Grant two more
> before he leaves us,
> like Diplomacy
> and Tact.
>
> Anon.

The second speaks for itself:

> Lord, on whom all love depends,
> Let me make and keep good friends:
> Bless me also with the patience
> To endure my wife's relations.
>
> Anon.

The third indicates that the granting of a prayer to one person may not suit another:

> The Duke of Rutland urged *The Times* to pray
> For rain: the rain came down the following day.
> The pious marvelled: the sceptics murmured: 'Fluke!'
> And farmers, late with hay, said: 'Damn that Duke!'
>
> Anon.

Another verse also reflects on conflicting petitions:

> The farmer prays for rain,
> The washerman for sun,
> If prayers were not in vain,
> The work would be undone.
>
> Anon.

✑✑✑

Help me, O Lord, always to give 100% at work: 12% on Monday; 23% on Tuesday; 40% on Wednesday; 20% on Thursday; and 5% on Friday.

✑✑✑

Dear God, may I remember, day by day, especially on dark days, when it seems that people are deliberately trying to annoy me, that it takes 42 muscles to frown, 28 to smile and only 4 to extend my arm and smack someone in the mouth.

✑✑✑

Teach me, good Lord, to be careful of the toes that I might step on today as they may be connected to the feet I may have to kiss tomorrow.

∾∾∾

The following is an anonymous prayer said with feeling and a certain amount of optimism:

> Dear Lord,
> So far today I have done very well. I have not lost my temper;
> I have not been greedy; no malicious gossip has passed my lips;
> I have hurt no one; I have not been vain nor conceited.
> I am glad to have done all these things on my own.
> But in a few minutes, O Lord, I am going to get up out of bed and go to work,
> and from that point on I will need all the help that I can get.

∾∾∾

O God, grant me the servility to forget the people I never liked anyway; the good fortune to remember the ones I do; and the eyesight to know the difference.   Anon.

Prayer of a Property Profiteer

On Sunday, Lord, a Mrs. Drew
Is coming here the house to view
Which is of course for sale.
Grant Thou, O Lord, that she forbear
From standing long upon the stair
That is, alas! too frail.

O do not let her hand draw back
The curtain and reveal the crack

Along the window-pane!
O guide her as she comes and goes,
So that no smell assails her nose
From the adjacent drain.

Let her not see the neighbouring slum
As she approaches. May she come
Along the better road,
And grant that she may, in a trice
Agree to the inflated price
We ask for our abode.

And grant, O Lord, to us who plead,
These favours that we may succeed
In what we now devise;
And through thine all-embracing love
Be made eternal tenants of
Thy mansion in the skies.

Harley Quinn[7]

A Prayer for Civil Servants

O Thou who seest all things below,
Grant that thy servants may go slow,
That they may study to comply
With regulations till they die.

Teach us, O Lord, to reverence
Committees more than common sense;
To train our minds to make no plan
And pass the baby when we can.

So when the temper seeks to give
Us feelings of initiative,
Or when alone we go too far,
Chastise us with a circular.

'Mid war and tumult, fire and storms,
Give strength, O Lord, to deal with forms.

Thus may thy servants ever be
A flock of perfect sheep for thee.

Anon.[8]

To God the embattled nations sing and shout,
'Gott strafe England' and 'God save the King'.
God this, God that and God the other thing.
'Good God,' said God, 'I've got my work cut out.'

Sir John Squire in 1914[9]

❧❧❧

Moses Reid, the evangelical Rector of Coppenhall from 1869 to 1880, used to ride around to pray at the farms at Rogationtide. At one farm, where the farmer was lazy, Reid said to his coachman: 'Drive on, John, these fields need muck, not prayers.'

❧❧❧

In a congregation in the Deep South of the United States they were praying to Jesus about a heavy church debt. Suddenly the old pastor interrupted: 'No, Lawd, don' sen' de blessed Jesus. Come right down Yo'self. Dis ain't no boy's job.'

❧❧❧

May the roof above never fall in,
May we below never fall out.

Anon.

❧❧❧

The following prayer is attributed to a Member of Parliament for Weymouth in 1727: 'O Lord, thou knowest that I have nine houses in the City of London, and that I have lately purchased an estate in Essex; I beseech thee to preserve the two counties of Middlesex and Essex from fires and earthquakes.'

In the same vein was part of a prayer quoted by Dean Ramsay: 'O Lord, we thank thee for the abundance and safe in-gathering of all our harvest except for a few fields between here and Stonehaven . . .'

We smile at the charming directness of this gypsy prayer:

> O my God, to still my longing,
>   Give me a mantle fine,
> Gaily trimmed with metal buttons
>   In the golden light to shine.
>
> Grant me, too, a goodly wife,
>   In her jacket, clean and neat,
> Arms of slender willow grace,
>   Flowerlike beauty in her feet.
>
> Laughing eyes, like seed of grape,
>   Shapely shoulders, like white bread,
> Lips as fresh as buds that burst
>   Into shining blossoms red.

Transylvanian gypsy song

5 *In the Pulpit*

SERMONS

If we are all laughing together, we are all seeing something
from the same point of view. Nothing, in my experience,
puts a speaker more en rapport with his audience than
successful humour. This rapport is something which is
essential for a preacher to establish.

Ian Dunlop in *Church Times*

෴

Anthony Trollope in *Barchester Towers* presented a more cynical
view of preaching:

There is perhaps no greater hardship at present inflicted
on mankind in civilised and free countries, than the necessity of listening to sermons. No one but a preaching clergyman has, in these realms, the power of compelling an
audience to sit silent and be tormented. No one but a
preaching clergyman can revel in platitudes, truisms and
untruisms, and yet receive, as his undisputed privilege, the
same respectful demeanour as though words of im-
passioned eloquence or persuasive logic, fell from his lips.[1]

෴

A verger at St Mary's, Oxford, the University Church, is reported
to have said: 'I have heard every sermon here for the past thirty
years, and, thank God, I am still a Christian.'

∿∿∿

Samuel Johnson had this to say: 'A woman's preaching is like a dog's walking on his hinder legs. It is not done well; but you are surprised to find it done at all.'[2]

∿∿∿

'I hope,' one visiting preacher said to the vicar, 'that I did not weary you with the length of my sermon.'

'No, indeed,' answered the vicar, 'nor by its depth either.'

∿∿∿

It was reported that Parson Pike of Kirby Malory in Leicestershire was so fat that he had to be winched in and out of his pulpit from an ingenious pulley by a local corn-merchant.

∿∿∿

A visitor to a Cardiff church admired the altar flowers. The verger agreed about their beauty. He then added: 'On Sunday nights they are always given to those who are sick after the sermon.'

∿∿∿

Relationships in the Chapter of St Paul's Cathedral have often been notoriously antagonistic. There is a story, probably apocryphal, that Canon Simpson once interrupted Dean W. R. Inge during a Christmas Day sermon. He answered the rhetorical question, 'Perhaps you are wondering when I am coming to the subject of our festival?' with a hearty, 'I do.' Inge, in fact, always spoke to the point. (For more about him, see chapter 7.)

∿∿∿

A country vicar once asked the Duke of Wellington if there was anything he wished the sermon to be about. 'Yes,' answered the Iron Duke, 'about ten minutes.'

∾∾∾

John Pentland Mahaffy, Provost of Trinity College, Dublin, was an outstanding academic, wit and somewhat eccentric clergyman. One Sunday the preacher in the college chapel asked him what he thought of the sermon. Mahaffy replied that it seemed to him like the peace and mercy of God. 'It was like the peace of God because it passed all understanding, and like his mercy because it showed every sign of enduring for ever.'

∾∾∾

John Jackson, who later became Bishop of London, told how, when preaching in the Chapel Royal of St James's, he was alerted to the presence of the Duke of Wellington in the congregation by the curious conduct of the verger. At the close of the sermon, he opened the door of the pulpit, and, just as the preacher was about to step through, suddenly closed it with all his force, and with a noise which rang through the building. 'I looked at him for an explanation,' the bishop continued, 'and he informed me in a whisper that his Grace the Duke of Wellington was asleep, and that, not liking to touch him, they adopted this method of rousing him from his slumbers. There was no necessity to repeat the bombardment, as "that good gray head", which all men knew, "was no longer nodding".'

∾∾∾

Charles Spurgeon, the great Baptist preacher, insisted on hearing the sermons of his assistant ministers before they preached to a congregation. A particularly nervous assistant delivered his effort in Spurgeon's study. When he came to a close there was a long and total silence.

'Will it do?' the young man eventually ventured.

'Will it do what?' he was answered.

❧❧❧

Many anecdotes about preachers seem too good to be true, especially where coincidence is concerned.

It is related that there was a vicar of Ashby in Leicestershire, who was so short that he needed a stool in the pulpit in order to be visible to his congregation. One day he chose a text from the Gospel of John: 'A little while ye shall see me, again a little while and ye shall not see me.' As soon as he had announced the text the stool collapsed.

One anecdote that comes in various forms concerns a curate who was asked to preach his first sermon at short notice. His opening words were reportedly: 'In the absence of our beloved vicar, I can only speak with whatever words are put on my lips by divine grace. Next week I hope to give you something much more worthy of your consideration.'

Along the same lines, a curate was asked to deputize for the bishop at the last moment. Afterwards, in the vestry, he apologized to the vicar's warden for his poor sermon. The warden answered: 'Don't worry, you did your best. It's those who sent you who should be shot.'

❧❧❧

'Well,' said a church warden to his vicar, after the vicar had spoken against atheism in very obscure terms, 'that was a fine sermon. But if I might make so bold as to say it, I still believe there is a God.'

❧❧❧

John Wesley, as a rule, did not allow fires in his chapel. He thought that if they were crowded with devotional people, there would be warmth enough in the building. A young minister was one day asked by his congregation to allow a stove to be placed in the church. 'But you did not ask for this in the time of my predecessor,' he said. 'Ah! sir,' was the reply, 'the case was different then, and there was a good fire in the pulpit.'

❧❧❧

It has been claimed that a 'know-all' is a misfit in the pulpit. A 'know-all', however, is a misfit anywhere. Those who make that claim should be aware that the great preachers of the Church have been nobody's fools. The pulpit should never be associated with anti-intellectualism.

John Wesley, a bookman if ever there was one, once famously torpedoed anti-intellectualism. A critic wrote to tell him that the Lord could do without Wesley's book learning. Wesley replied that he was aware already that the Lord could do without his learning and that he could also do without the ignorance of his correspondent.

❧❧❧

In a sermon at Rugby School the Reverend Edward Meyrick Goulburn (1818–97) said: 'Let the scintillations of your wit be like the coruscations of summer lightning, lambent but innocuous.'[3]

❧❧❧

Edward Stillingfleet (1635–99), the Bishop of Worcester, once stood up daringly to his monarch, Charles II. The King had asked him why he read his sermons before him, but preached without book elsewhere. The Bishop replied that preaching before so great an audience made him distrust his own abilities.

'But', he asked in return, 'how is it that your Majesty reads your speeches in Parliament, having no such reason?'

'Why,' said the King, 'the truth is, I have asked my subjects so often for so much money, that I am really ashamed to look them in the face.'

❧❧❧

A preacher called Bourdaloue came to the court of Louis XIV to give the Lenten sermons in the chapel at Versailles. His sermons stirred the congregation, but were delivered at great speed and at great length. Certain ladies who were not sure that they could contain themselves until the end of the service would arrive with a small china receptacle, known as a Bourdaloue, concealed under their voluminous skirts.

∾∾∾

History shows us that there has always been a strong, but not always rewarding, relationship between the monarchy and the church.

On one occasion, Fénélon, the French theologian and Archbishop of Cambrai, and a priest were the only people in the congregation, usually numerous, when King Louis XIV arrived.

'What is the reason for all this?' asked the monarch.

'Why,' replied Fénélon, 'I caused it to be announced that your Majesty would not attend divine service today, that you might know, sire, who came to worship God, and who to flatter the king.'

This anecdote may not show Fénélon and the priest up in a good light. Had their preaching made only such a superficial impact in court circles?

King Charles II once dismissed both the preacher and his congregation with this curt remark: 'His nonsense suits their nonsense.'

One of the first acts performed by George III, after his accession to the throne, was to issue an order prohibiting any of the clergy who should be called to preach before him, from paying him any compliment in their discourses. His Majesty was led to this from the fulsome adulation which Dr Thomas Wilson, prebendary of Westminster, thought proper to deliver in the Chapel Royal: and for which, instead of thanks, he received from his royal auditor a pointed reprimand, his Majesty observing 'that he came to chapel to hear the praises of God, and not his own'.

On 3 August 1896, Sir Henry Ponsonby sent the following letter to R. T. Davidson, then Dean of Windsor, on behalf of Queen Victoria:

The Queen tells me to let you know that she was well
pleased with the sermon preached by the poor but prolific —. I am to add that on the previous Sunday R.
preached a long and most tedious rambling discourse. He
lost his place, repeated himself, and Her Majesty thought
it would never end. She cannot let him preach again,
though if you consider it necessary he may read the service
here.

It is amusing to note that Queen Victoria remarked that she had
never known a bishop whose preaching had not deteriorated after
his consecration. No doubt she would have excluded her favourite
bishop, Boyd-Carpenter, from this censure.

∾∾∾

In a letter to his father, written when he was an undergraduate
at St John's College, Oxford, and dated 12 February 1878, A. E.
Housman not only mentioned the length of Canon King's sermon
when he preached at St Mary's, but went on to illustrate the importance of personality when preaching:

The sermon was unconscionably long, and considerably
over our heads, brimming as it did with patristic learning,
until, at the end of an hour and a quarter, he concluded
with an apology to his younger brethren for having bored
them, and giving as his reason that Our Lord grieved Peter,
which I did not quite see the force of.

Housman continued:

But I felt it was quite worth sitting still for an hour and
a quarter to watch such an interesting personality. He is
tall, but stoops; and haggard in the face but without grey
hair; and his sermon was most masterly here and there.
The exquisitely deprecating way and affected timidity with
which he put his strongest points, and the mournful and
apologetic modulation of his voice where he was pulling
Dean Stanley to pieces, were really most worthy of Disraeli,

and not altogether unlike, were it not for the deadly earnest, which was rather detrimental to the oratorical effect.[4]

∾∾∾

Sir Joshua Reynolds praised Mudge's sermons.

JOHNSON: 'Mudge's sermons are good, but not practical. He grasps more sense than he can hold; he takes more corn than he can make into meal; he opens a wide prospect, but it is so distant that it is indistinct. I love Blair's sermons. Though the dog is a Scotchman, and a Presbyterian, and everything he should not be, I was the first to praise them. Such was my candour' (smiling). MRS. BOSCAWEN: 'Such his great merit to get the better of your prejudices.' JOHNSON: 'Why, Madam, let us compound the matter; let us ascribe it to my candour and his merit.'

James Boswell, Life of Samuel Johnson, 20 April, 1781

Archbishop Whately pronounced a classic criticism: 'Many a wandering discourse one hears in which the preacher aims at nothing and hits it.'

Margot Asquith, the wife of the Prime Minister, complained that modern sermons tend to be too secular. She said: 'It would be as surprising to hear God mentioned in one of them as to find a fox in a bus.'

∾∾∾

Three sermon criticisms from France:

In eighteenth-century France a Parisian, Sebastian Mercier, wrote: 'In more than one sermon lately the only things Christian were the sign of the cross and the Gospel citation.'

When a superior of the Lazarists, a certain Father Bonnet, preached in Nancy, one of the congregation offered to put a gold louis on each place in the text of his sermon where the name of Christ occurred.

Louis XIV, after listening to one sermon, remarked: 'If the good Abbé had spoken a little about religion today, I think that he would have mentioned everything.'

∾∾∾

One pompous preacher asked a member of the congregation what he thought of the sermon. He was told: 'Well, if you must know I did not like it.' 'Why was that?' asked the preacher, surprised at the blunt response. The chilling answer was: 'Firstly, you read it; secondly, you read it badly; and thirdly, it was not worth reading.'

Also on the subject of frank criticism, the following exchange is reported to have taken place between an unnamed clergyman and George Canning, the nineteenth-century politician.

Clergyman: 'How did you like my sermon, Mr. Canning?'
Canning: 'You were brief.'
Clergyman: 'Yes, you know I avoid being tedious.'
Canning: 'You *were* tedious.'

∾∾∾

According to Dr Eachard in his *Grounds and Occasions of the Contempt of the Clergy*, published about 1698, in the sermons of his day there was too much 'high tossing and swaggering, besprinkling all their sermons with plenty of Greek and Latin'. He continued: 'This Learned way of Talking tho' for the most part, is done meerly out of Ostentation, yet sometimes (which makes not the case much better) it is done in Compliment and Civility to the all-wise Patron, or all-understanding Justice of the Peace, in the Parish.'

∾∾∾

The last word on negative criticism must go to Mark Twain who said: 'He charged nothing for his preaching, and it was worth it too.'

SLEEP AND SERMONS

Over the centuries it appears that there were always long and tedious sermons which sent people to sleep in church. In the British Museum, a drawing by William Hogarth depicts a whole congregation sound asleep except for the sour-looking parish clerk and the parson who, although he is preaching, seems to be on the verge of slumber himself.

Some preachers resorted to making startling statements to shake their flocks awake. One is reputed to have shouted: 'Fire, fire!' 'Where, where?' some members of the congregation cried out. 'In hell,' responded the preacher, 'where all who sleep under the preaching of the Gospel will surely go.'

When Robert South preached before Charles II and his court, he noticed that not only the King but many of those about him were audibly sleeping. Lord Lauderdale, it seems, was snoring louder than anyone else. South broke off his sermon and said: 'My dear Lord Lauderdale, let me implore you not to snore so loud – you'll wake the King.'

∾∾∾

On 17 November 1661, Samuel Pepys noted that he 'slept best part of the sermon'.

Charles Churchill (1732–64), who was curate of Rainham in Essex and later at St John's Church, Smith Square, was proud to acknowledge the soporific power of his own preaching. 'Sleep at my bidding', he said, 'crept from pew to pew.'

> The ladies praise the curate's eyes –
> I never see their light divine;
> For when he prays he closes his,
> And when he preaches mine.
>   Anon.

∾∾∾

Sydney Smith said of himself: 'When I am in the pulpit, I have the pleasure of seeing my audience nod approbation while they sleep.'

Of one particularly boring preacher, he commented, 'He evidently thought sin was to be taken from man, as Eve was from Adam, by casting him into a deep sleep.'

Writing in the *Edinburgh Review* about the Reverend Dr Langford's *Anniversary Sermon* of the Royal Humane Society, Sydney Smith made this superb comment on the sermon under review:

> An incident which happened to the gentleman engaged in reviewing this Sermon, proves, in the most striking manner, the importance of this charity for restoring to life persons in whom the vital power is suspended. He was discovered with Dr. Langford's discourse lying open before him, in the state of the most profound sleep; from which he could not, by any means, be awakened for a great length of time. By attending, however, to the rules prescribed by the Humane Society, flinging in the smoke of tobacco, applying hot flannels, and carefully removing the discourse itself to a great distance, the critic was restored to his disconsolate brothers.

∾∾∾

Jonathan Swift made this dry comment about an incident recorded in the Acts of the Apostles, when a young man called Eutychus fell asleep and fell from a window-ledge when Saint Paul was preaching:

> The accident which happened to this young man in the text hath not been sufficient to discourage his successors; but because the preachers now in the world, however they may exceed St. Paul in the art of setting men to sleep, do extremely fall short of him in the working of miracles; therefore men are become so cautious, as to choose more safe and convenient stations and postures for taking their repose . . .

Swift's admirably succinct sermon on this incident is unsurpassable. He started: 'I have chosen these words with design, if possible, to disturb some part of this audience of half-an-hour's sleep, for the convenience and exercise whereof this place, at this season of the day, is very much celebrated.'

'Opium', he continued, 'is not so stupefying to many persons as an afternoon sermon.' He thought that the very sound of a sermon was enough to lull people's senses, 'because they all awake so very regularly as soon as it ceaseth and with much devotion receive the blessing, dozed and besotted with indecencies I am ashamed to repeat.' A scorner or unbeliever may eventually come to listen, 'but the sleeper shuts up all avenues to his soul; he is like the deaf adder that harkeneth not to the voice of the charmer, charm he never so wisely.'

The dull preacher may be partly to blame for the snoring in church, but Swift certainly took a mighty swipe at those who, 'after a gluttonous meal, their senses dozed and stupefied . . . retire to God's house to sleep out the afternoon . . .'

∾∾∾

Joseph Addison (1672–1719) was the son of the Dean of Lichfield and was educated at Charterhouse, where he first met Richard Steele, and Oxford. In March 1711 he and Steele brought out the first number of *The Spectator*, which featured the fictitious squire Sir Roger de Coverley. In the following charming passage Addison describes Sir Roger in church: in relation to sleep, he obviously had one standard for his tenants and another for himself.

> My friend Sir Roger, being a good churchman, has beauti-
> fied the inside of his church with several texts of his own
> choosing. He has likewise given a handsome pulpit-cloth,
> and railed in the communion table at his own expense.
> He has often told me, that at his coming to his estate he
> found his parishioners very irregular; and that in order to
> make them kneel and join in the responses, he gave every-
> one of them a hassock and a common-prayer book. At the
> same time he employed an itinerant singing master, who
> goes about the country for that purpose, to instruct them

rightly in the tunes of the psalms, upon which they now very much value themselves, and indeed outdo most of the country churches that I have heard.

As Sir Roger is landlord to the whole congregation, he keeps them in very good order, and will suffer nobody to sleep in it beside himself, for if by chance he has been surprised into a short nap at sermon, upon recovering out of it he stands up and looks about him, and if he sees anybody else nodding, either wakes them himself or sends his servants to them. Several other of the old knight's particularities break out upon these occasions: sometimes he will be lengthening out a verse in the singing-psalms, half a minute after the rest of the congregation have done with it. Sometimes, when he is pleased with the matter of his devotion, he pronounces *Amen* three or four times to the same prayer; and sometimes stands up when everybody else is upon their knees, to count the congregation, or see if any of his tenants are missing.[5]

∾∾∾

It is said that the good Hugh Latimer, the Bishop of Worcester who was martyred alongside Nicholas Ridley in 1555, was tolerant towards those who went to sleep during sermons. Latimer told a story about a gentlewoman of London whose neighbour met her in the street and asked: 'Mistress, whither go ye?'

'Marry,' said she, 'I am going to St Thomas of Acres to the sermon. I could not sleep all this last night and I am going now thither. I never failed of a good nap there.'

∾∾∾

At some churches, like that at Claverley in Shropshire, 'sluggard-walkers' were employed. Their job was to awaken those who fell asleep during sermons by tapping them on the head with a long pole. Sleeping women in the congregation were tickled under their noses so that their coiffures were not spoilt.

POLITICS IN THE PULPIT

The parson leaves the *Christian* in the lurch
Whene'er he brings his politics into Church.
John Byrom, *Epigrams*

In eighteenth-century England the pulpit was often used blatantly either for the Whig or the Tory cause. John Byrom spoke against this in a piece called 'On Clergymen Preaching Politics':

> Indeed, Sir Peter, I could wish, I own
> That parsons would let politics alone.
> Plead, if they will, the customary plea,
> For such like talk, when o'er a dish of tea:
> But when they tease us with it from the pulpit,
> I own, Sir Peter, that I cannot gulp it.

An advertisement appeared in the *Reading Mercury* in 1726 which declared political requirements plainly: 'Curate wanted who will have easy duty and a stipend of £50 per annum, besides valuable perquisites. He must be zealously affected to the present government . . .'

∾∾∾

In 1845, when Bishop Samuel Wilberforce took his seat in the House of Lords, Prince Albert gave him the following good advice:

> A bishop ought to abstain completely from mixing himself up with the politics of the day, and beyond giving a general support of the Queen's Government, should take no part in the discussion of state affairs . . . but he should come forward whenever the interests of humanity are at stake and give boldly and manfully his advice to House and country.

Putting politics in the pulpit can be a cheap and mediocre exercise. It takes no rigorous intellectual activity nor profound soul-searching

in order to parade on a Sunday morning one's own particular political prejudices. C. S. Lewis acidly commented that most political
sermons teach the congregation nothing except what newspapers
are taken in the vicarage. The case against mixing Church doctrine
with political opinion in the pulpit was classically and superbly put
by Edmund Burke in his *Reflections on the Revolution in France*,[6]
where he accused political preachers of being ignorant of 'the character they assume'. They do not know, in other words, what they are
talking about.

∾∾∾

When the Bishop of Salisbury interfered over the Catholic Emanci-
pation Bill, Arthur Wellesley, the Duke of Wellington, wrote to him:

> As your Lordship is so kind as to give me your advice
> allow me to give you a little: that is to reside in your
> Diocese; to attend to the duties of your High, Important
> and Sacred Office ... and Your Lordship may rely upon
> that it will do more to prevent the establishment of Popery
> and Dissent ... than ... by your Political writing.

> The Bishop of Chester preached before the King and made
> a great flattering sermon which I did not like, that clergy
> should meddle in matters of state.   Samuel Pepys, *Diary*

Praying, as well as preaching, can be directed along party political
lines. One such prayer went:

> O Lord, we ask Thee for a Governor who would rule
> in the fear of God; who would defeat the ringleaders of
> corruption, enhance the prosperity of the State, promote
> the happiness of the people – O Lord, what's the use of
> beating about the bush? Give us George W. Briggs for
> Governor! Amen.

It is enough, it is a very great deal, it is the priority that people,
after hearing Christian preaching, should become good and continue

being good. Injecting sermons with political points does not advance that aim. The Quaker William Penn (1644–1718), the founder of Pennsylvania, wrote:

> Though good laws do well, good men do better. Governments, like clocks, go from the motion men give them, and as governments are made and moved by men, so by them they are ruined too. Wherefore governments rather depend on men than men upon governments. Let men be good and the government cannot be bad; if it be ill they will cure it. But, if men be bad, let the government be ever so good, they will endeavour to warp and spoil it to their turn.

T. B. Macaulay wrote a marvellous passage exposing the absurdity of preachers who try to force contemporary political conditions into the pages of the Bible. The setting was the coronation of King James II. Macaulay wrote:

> Francis Turner, Bishop of Ely, preached. He was one of those writers who still affected the obsolete style of Archbishop Williams and Bishop Andrews. The sermon was made up of quaint conceits, such as seventy years earlier might have been admired, but such as moved the scorn of a generation accustomed to the purer eloquence of Sprat, of South, and of Tillotson. King Solomon was King James. Adonijah was Monmouth. Joab was a Rye House conspirator; Shimei, a Whig libeller; Abiathar, an honest but misguided old Cavalier. One phrase in the Book of Chronicles was construed to mean that the King was above the Parliament: and another was cited to prove that he alone ought to command the militia. Towards the close of the discourse the orator very timidly alluded to the new and embarrassing position in which the Church stood with reference to the sovereign, and reminded his hearers that the Emperor Constantius Chlorus, though not himself a Christian, had held in honour those Christians who remained true to their religion, and had treated with scorn

those who sought to earn his favour by apostasy. The service in the Abbey was followed by a stately banquet in the Hall, the banquet by brilliant fireworks, and the fireworks by much bad poetry.[7]

> How small, of all that human hearts endure,
> That part which laws or kings can cause or cure!
>
> Samuel Johnson

The last and perfect word on the subject.

6   *Concerning the Clergy*

THE CLERGY

The Clergy is the collective body of men and women ordained as ministers of the Church or Clerks in Holy Orders. Clerks were those who could read and write. This ability was so largely confined to priests that in the Middle Ages a person could save himself from hanging by claiming to be tried by the ecclesiastical courts rather than the King's courts if he could recite a verse from the Psalms known as the 'neck verse'. Clergymen have traditionally worn various forms of clerical dress, the most obvious feature of which has been, since the nineteenth century, the clerical 'dog' collar. Their distinctive attire has made them a visible aspect of the Church.

English social history would have been impoverished without the lives of the clergy, the parish priests in particular. There are many tributes to them, notably in prose but also in poetry, including verses in the Prologue of Geoffrey Chaucer's *The Canterbury Tales* and in Oliver Goldsmith's *The Deserted Village*.

ღღღ

The following is a description of the clergy ordained in the early years of the reign of Queen Elizabeth I. After the disruptive reformations and violent reversals of the two previous reigns, Elizabeth was trying to settle opposite elements, a process known as the Elizabethan Settlement. According to this passage the new clergy were a very mixed bunch that included some witty performers:

First we may note how many were men of occupation, late entrants to the ministry out of some other trade or calling, of which the surveys specify thirty-four, including those of girthmaker, harper, and sow-gelder, as well as any number of tailors and weavers. A survey of the same parishes fifty years later would have revealed a clergy with a more respectable and homogenous background. But the surveys provide additional evidence that after ordination the clergy continued to be men of a variety of aptitudes, frequently involved in agriculture, more rarely in industry, and sometimes pursuing interests of a specialised nature. The chief trade of the aged and barely literate Vicar of Grafton in Warwickshire was to cure hawks that are hurt or diseased 'for which purpose manie do usuallie repaire to him'. As for the Vicar of Lanteglos, he was simply 'the best Wrastler in Cornewall'. Elsewhere in these documents we meet working physicians, surveyors, dealers in livestock, and money-lenders, as well as several 'jesters'. For a proportion of the Elizabethan clergy seem to have been, to all intents and purposes, professional entertainers, like William Glibery, vicar of Halstead, described as a 'verie ridiculous preacher', whose witty but gross performance in the pulpit was lovingly recorded by his scandalised neighbours. Others, like their eighteenth-century descendants, made a living out of clandestine marriages. But the vicar of Warwick was a mere scholar, 'learned in the tongues, yet the people profit not'.   Patrick Collinson[1]

There have been comic criticisms of the clergy as a class. The clergyman and historian Thomas Fuller (1608–61) complained that families in England encouraged only their intellectually and physically weakest male offspring to become clergymen. He wrote of 'many nowadays, who begrutch their pregnant [intellectually promising] children to God's service, reserving straight timber to be beams in other buildings, and only condemning crooked pieces for the temple; so that what is found unfit for city, camp or court (not to add ship or shop) is valued worth enough for the Church.'

The sloth, in its wild state, spends its life in trees, and never leaves them but from force or accident. The eagle to the sky, the mole to the ground, the sloth to the tree; but what is most extraordinary, he lives not upon the branches, but under them. He moves suspended, rests suspended, sleeps suspended, and passes his life in suspense like a young clergyman distantly related to a bishop.   Sydney Smith

In the late nineteenth and twentieth centuries 'bollocks' came to be a word for nonsense. From the seventeenth century until the late nineteenth century 'bollocks' or 'ballocks' was a slang term for a clergyman. In 1864 the Officer Commanding the Straights Fleet always referred to his chaplain as Ballocks. Bollocks gradually came to mean rubbish because it was considered that clergymen spoke so much of it during their sermons.

∾∾∾

An American wit of the twentieth century, Robert Benchley, finely summed up the existence of clergymen: 'Work for the Lord. The pay is terrible, but the fringe benefits are out of this world.'

The clergy are as like as peas: I cannot tell them apart.
                                        R. W. Emerson

In my opinion, parsons are very like other men, and neither the better nor the worse for wearing a black gown or white surplice.   Earl of Chesterfield

As the French say, there are three sexes – men, women, and clergymen.   Sydney Smith

The Church and clergy here, no doubt
        Are very near a-kin:
    Both weather-beaten are without;
        And empty both within.
                            Jonathan Swift

On a Clergyman's Horse Biting Him

The Steed bit his master;
    How came this to pass?
He heard the good pastor
    Cry, All flesh is grass.

Anon.

His creed no parson ever knew,
For this was still his 'simple plan',
To have with clergymen to do
As little as a Christian can.

Sir Francis Doyle

Clergymen often remained in office into extreme old age in times when there were no regulations about retirement and no adequate pensions on which to retire. There have been those who suffered from more or less acute senile loss of memory. They muddled their notices and lost their place in services, forgot names and arrived at wrong times. Many were excused for having their minds on higher things.

Social isolation may have led to an incipient eccentricity becoming a rampant quirkiness among some of them. Many certainly gained a notorious reputation for being absent-minded. In a few cases they seemed to elevate their disability into a fine art.

Such a person was the sporting clergyman, the Reverend George Harvest (1728–89) of Thames Ditton. His parishioners did not help him with his affliction of absent-mindedness. He used to read his sermons. Some members of his parish found his sermon notes lying on the pulpit lectern and jumbled them up. There were a few moments of hilarity when he read them out as he had found them, but the sermon proved even drearier than usual, and the people began to slip out of church, one by one, until by the end he was alone.

On another occasion a verse was slipped amongst the banns to be read on a particular Sunday. Again, George Harvest, abstractedly, simply read out what was in front of him:

> I publish the Banns of Marriage between
> Jack Cheshire and the widow Gleen,
> 'Twixt Oxford here and Paternoster,
> Who to keep out wind and weather,
> So if you wish to put in caveat
> Now is the time to have it at.

As a young man he was engaged to a daughter of the Bishop of London, but he went gudgeon-fishing on the wedding day and was too late for the ceremony. The offended lady, not surprisingly, broke off the match.

He frequently forgot the times of services and would walk into church with his gun to see why people were assembled. He was extremely negligent in his dress. Sometimes he would buy a penny-worth of shrimps, and put them in his waistcoat pocket among 'tobacco, worms, gentles for fishing and other trumpery'.

> One day Lady Onslow, being desirous of knowing the most remarkable planets and constellations, requested Mr. Harvest, on a fine starlit night, to point them out to her, which he undertook to do; but in the midst of his lecture, having occasion to make water, thought that he need not interrupt it, and accordingly directing that operation with one hand, went on in his explanation, pointing out the constellations with the other. From *The Olio*, 1796

From a letter sent to what was then called 'The Ministry of Pensions': 'Can't you do anything for Mrs X? She has no clothes and is visited regularly by the clergy.'

∽∽∽

In seeking promotion or preferment some clergymen have adopted extraordinary strategies. One, in preaching before Lord North when he was Prime Minister, is said to have chosen for his text Psalm 75: 7–8: 'For promotion cometh neither from the East, nor from the West: nor yet from the South. And why? God is the Judge: he putteth down one, and setteth up another'.

To a Literary Critic

I would not have you scorn archdeaconships,
　　　Or comfortable deaneries refuse;
Yet should I mourn, did these things quite eclipse
　　　Your mild and worthy Muse.
Nor shall I watch incurious your career;
　　　For though your heart on things above be set,
You lack not gifts such as avail us here,
　　　And may reach Lambeth yet.
　　　　　　　　　　　Sir William Watson, *Retrogression*

I could name some gentlemen of the gown, whose awkward, spruce, prim, sneering, and smirking countenances,
the very tone of their voices, and an ungainly strut in
their walk, without one single talent for any office, have
contrived to get good preferment by the mere force of
flattery and cringing.　　　　　　　　Jonathan Swift

The Reverend George Gilfillan has the distinction of being the subject
of the first 'masterpiece' of William McGonagall (1825–1902), who
achieved fame as probably the worst poet to write in English. These
excruciating verses praised the mind and eloquence of the clergyman:

　　　Rev George Gilfillan of Dundee,
　　　There is none can you excel;
　　　You have boldly rejected the Confession of Faith,
　　　And defended your cause right well.

　　　The first time I heard him speak,
　　　'Twas in the Kinnaird hall,
　　　Lecturing on the Garibaldi movement,
　　　As loud as he could bawl.

The eighteenth-century poet Thomas Gray wrote the following lines
on a clergyman whom he described as 'a meddling impudent cleric'.
He was so vile that even the Devil was tempted to become a
clergyman;

Such Tophet was; so looked the grinning fiend
Whom many a frightened prelate called his friend;
I saw them bow and, while they wished him dead,
with servile simper nod the mitred head.
Our Mother-Church with half-averted sight
Blushed as she blessed her grisly proselyte;
Hosannahs rung through Hell's tremendous borders,
and Satan's self had thoughts of taking orders.

The Reverend Robert Hewitt

I march'd three miles through scorching sand,
With zeal in heart, and notes in hand;
I rode four more to Great St. Mary,
Using four legs, when two were weary:
To three fair virgins I did tie men,
In the close bonds of pleasing Hymen;
I dipp'd two babes in holy water,
And purefied their mother after.
Within an hour and eke a half,
I preach'd three congregations deaf;
Where, thundering out, with lungs long winded,
I chopped so fast, that few were minded.
My emblem, the laborious sun,
Saw all these mighty labours done
Before one race of his was run.
All this perform'd by Robert Hewitt:
What mortal else could e'er go through it!

Jonathan Swift[2]

ARCHBISHOPS AND BISHOPS

Bishops have been figures of fun and the targets of witticisms in part because of the extraordinary attire that they chose to wear. Now they have at least shed their episcopal gaiters.

In part it is because humour always enters the gap between things as they are and as they should be. Bishops have been affluent and powerful. Their position and wealth has often led to arrogance. A vain teacher of Christianity is inherently ridiculous – a balloon waiting to be pricked. The diary of Samuel Pepys is full of criticisms of the episcopacy; and it was said, in 1641, that they who hated bishops 'hated them worse than the devil; and they who loved them did not love them as well as their own dinner'.

They also become vulnerable to comic asides when they bend over backwards to be all things to all men and pretend to agree with everyone. This can only be done by a person with no mind of their own. It is dangerous to walk only in the middle of the road; one is likely to get run over there.

They were and are also vulnerable when they set themselves up as monuments of moral respectability. This is why there are all those 'As the Bishop said to the Actress' or 'As the Actress said to the Bishop' remarks. The slightest linguistic slip, lapse or double entendre is then blown out of all proportion.

The traffic has not all been one way and some bishops, like William Temple, have been amusing men who made comic remarks, often at the expense of their priests.

∾∾∾

One bishop was noted for the brevity of his sermons and his taciturn conversation. The Mayoress of his home town was once entertaining him, but gave up in despair her attempts to engage him in conversation. 'Some tea, bishop?' 'No tea.' 'Some coffee, bishop?' 'No coffee.' 'Some whiskey and soda, bishop?' 'No soda.'

∾∾∾

Sydney Smith's witticisms about bishops are the best of all.[3] They include:

> I have, alas, only one illusion left, and that is the Archbishop of Canterbury.

I must believe in the Apostolic Succession there being no other way of tracing the Bishop of Exeter to Judas Iscariot.

What bishops like in their clergy is a drooping-down-deadness of manner.

Can a bishop marry? How can he flirt? The most he can say is – I will see you in the vestry after the service.

Bishops are men; not always the wisest of men: not always preferred for eminent virtues and talents, or for whatever good reason whatever known to the public. They are almost always devoid of striking and indecorous vices; but a man may be very shallow, very arrogant, and very vindictive, though a bishop; and pursue with unrelenting hatred a subordinate clergyman, whose principles he dislikes and whose genius he fears.

❧❧❧

Dean W. R. Inge said of one bishop, who had held on to his office for far too long, that he had 'every Christian quality save that of resignation'. He also remarked that when an evangelical is made a bishop, the transformation is 'even more rapid than that of a Labour Member who is made a peer'.

He said of an Archbishop that he took 'a first class single ticket on the line of least resistance'.

A bishop keeps on saying at eighty what he was told to say at eighteen. *Oscar Wilde*

Archbishop: A Christian ecclesiastic of a rank superior to that attained by Christ. *H. L. Menken*

The Archbishop of Canterbury, the Archbishop of York and the Bishop of Durham hold their offices by 'Divine Providence'. All other English bishops hold them by 'Divine Permission'. Herbert

Hensley Henson, himself the Bishop of Durham, commented that some of them did so by 'Divine Inadvertence'.

∾∾∾

One Archbishop of Armagh was so cold in manner that he was nicknamed the 'Marble Arch'.

∾∾∾

The poet John Milton held a jaundiced view of bishops whom he described as 'A pure elixir of mischief, pestilent alike to all, a sad and doleful succession of illiterate and blind guides'.

> 'It was a blonde. A blonde to make a bishop kick a hole in a stained-glass window.'
>
> Raymond Chandler in *Farewell, My Lovely*

A Quarrelsome Bishop

> To hide her ordure, claws the cat;
> You claw, but not to cover that.
> Be decenter, and learn at least
> One lesson from the cleanlier beast.
>
> Walter Savage Landor

> Now hear an allusion: a mitre, you know,
> is divided above, but united below.
> If this you consider, our emblem is right;
> the bishops divide, but the clergy unite.
>
> Jonathan Swift[4]

On Gilbert Glanvill, Bishop of Rochester

> Gilbertus Glanvill, whose heart was as hard as an anvil,
> Always litigious when he should have been highly
>   religious,

Still charged with lawsuits he to that court aptly
    descended
Where quiet appears not and quarrels never are ended.

Matthew Prior

William Warburton, Bishop of Gloucester

He was so proud that should he meet
The Twelve Apostles in the street
He'd turn his nose up at them all
And shove his Saviour from the wall.

Charles Churchill

On Cardinal Wolsey

Begot by Butchers, but by Bishops bred,
How high his honour holds his haughty head.

Anon.

There was an Archbishop of Kent
Whose nose was remarkably bent.
    One day, they suppose,
    He just followed his nose,
And nobody knows where he went.

Anon.

The diarist Chips Channon reported that following a visit to Wells
Cathedral he had lunch at the Palace with the Bishop of Bath &
Wells. Conversation got around to Barchester, and the Bishop
announced, to everyone's consternation: 'There is nothing I like
better than to lie on my bed for an hour with my favourite Trollope.'[5]

∾∾∾

Henry Colville Montgomery Campbell was Bishop of London in the
1950s. He had a reputation for a sardonic sense of humour. At his
enthronement in 1956 there was some delay at the door of St Paul's

Cathedral in answering his ceremonial knock on it. He remarked to his chaplain: 'Do you think that we have come to the right place?' When he saw all the aged clergy inside the cathedral, he said: 'The see gives up its dead.'

An elderly clergyman was caught by Campbell escaping from a religious retreat to visit the local shops. 'You see, my Lord,' he stammered out, 'I am breaking my retreat, but I have consulted the Holy Spirit and have been guided to do some shopping.' 'How odd,' answered the bishop, 'that you should both be wrong: this happens to be early closing day.'

He once had to decline an invitation to give an after-dinner speech. He was asked to recommend a wit who could make an entertaining speech in his place. The bishop said that he did not know of one, but added that he knew of several half-wits in his diocese and wondered if two would do instead.

∾∾∾

Henry Phillpotts (1778–1869), who was Bishop of Exeter from 1830 to 1869, had a beautiful villa near Torquay. A lady who visited him gushingly exclaimed: 'What a lovely spot this is, Bishop! It is so Swiss!' 'Yes, ma'am,' Phillpotts blandly replied, 'it is very Swiss; only there is no sea in Switzerland, and there are no mountains here.'

∾∾∾

William Boyd-Carpenter, who was Bishop of Ripon between 1884 and 1911, was once heckled by a man who shouted, 'Do you really believe that Jonah was swallowed by a whale?'

'When I get to heaven I will ask him,' the Bishop said.

'And suppose he isn't there?' his questioner persisted.

'In that case,' the Bishop answered, 'you will have to ask him yourself.'

∾∾∾

Dr Potter, the Episcopalian Bishop of New York, was once asked by a lady at a dinner party why in pictures and statues of angels they are always depicted as women or as young men without beards or moustaches. He answered: 'Everyone knows that women naturally inherit the Kingdom of Heaven, but the men only get in by a very close shave.'

∾∾∾

Bishops could be very dismissive in their missives or letters. Sydney Smith said that he had never met with any style 'so entirely clear of all redundant and vicious ornament' as that adopted by the Lord Bishop of Peterborough towards his clergy. Smith claimed that it could be reduced to: 'Reverend Sir, I shall do what I please. Peterborough.'

In so far as brevity is the soul of wit, some brief answers from bishops were witty. Others were simply impolite. The Duke of York wrote to the Protestant Bishop of Cork about a man called Ponsonby. The duke wanted him to be made a clergyman. He therefore wrote: 'Dear Cork, Ordain Ponsonby. Yours, York.' The bishop replied: 'Dear York, Ponsonby ordained. Cork.'

A clergyman once made the mistake of quoting St Ambrose of Milan in a letter to Bishop Blomfield on a matter of ritual. He got this frosty answer: 'Sir, St Ambrose was not Bishop of London; I am. Your truly, W Lond.'

When one of the clergy of Bishop Thorold wrote to him to ask permission to make a long journey in the East, he was told: 'Dear —, Go to Jericho. Yours, Thorold.' Jericho, a scorching hot town, was often used as a euphemism for 'Hell'.

Charles Gore was once the Vicar of Radley in the Diocese of Oxford. He sent his bishop, William Stubbs, a huge plan on how the diocese should be reorganized. He received for his pains this postcard by return: 'Dear Gore, Don't be a bore.' When Kenneth Kirk, another Bishop of Oxford, was invited to preach somewhere, he also answered on a postcard: 'OK, KO' (Kenneth Oxon).

A poverty-stricken vicar wrote to his bishop to complain about a flooded cellar in the vicarage. He wrote: 'My poor hens that lived down there are all drowned.' The bishop solved the problem in two words: 'Keep ducks.'

When the Reverend Robert Taylor applied for a living to Dr Buckner, Bishop of Chichester, in 1818, he got this curt rebuff: 'My dear Taylor, the background is the place for you.'

∿∿∿

Richard Corbet, Bishop of Norwich

Richard Corbet, D.D., deane of Christchurch, 1620; bishop of Oxon, 1628; bishop of Norwich, 1632 ... He was very facetious, and a good fellowe ... After he was D. of Divinity, he sung ballads at the Crosse at Abingdon on a market-day ... The jolly Doctor putts-off his gowne, and putts-on the ballad singer's leathern jacket, and being a handsome man, and had a rare full voice, he presently vended a great many, and had a great audience ...

His conversation was extreme pleasant, Dr. Stubbins was one of his cronies; he was a jolly fatt Dr. and a very good housekeeper; parson in Oxforshire. As Dr. Corbet and he were riding in Lob-lane, in wett weather, ('tis an extraordinary deepe dirty lane) the coach fell; and Dr. Corbet sayd that Dr. Stubbins was up to the elbowes in mud, he was up to the elbowes in Stubbins.

... His chaplain, Dr. Lushington, was a very learned and ingeniose man, and they loved one another. The bishop sometimes would take the key of the wine-cellar, and he and his chaplaine would goe and lock themselves in and be merry. Then first he layes down his episcopall hat, – 'There lyes the Dr.' Then putts off his gowne, – 'There lyes the Bishop.' Then 'twas, – 'Here's to thee, Corbet', and 'Here's to thee, Lushington.'

He built a pretty house near the Cawsey beyond Friar

Bacon's studie. He married [Alice Hutton] whom 'twas said he begott. She was a very beautifull woman, and so was her mother . . .   John Aubrey, *Brief Lives*[6]

✺✺✺

Cosmo Gordon Lang, who was Archbishop of Canterbury from 1928 to 1942, was a comic figure for all the wrong reasons. He was the butt for the humour of men with barbed tongues who were expert in dipping their pens in vitriol.

When King Edward VIII abdicated in 1936, he was strongly criticized by Archbishop Lang. The Archbishop received the following anonymous verse through the post:

> My Lord Archbishop, what a scold you are!
> And when your man is down how bold you are!
> And, auld Lang Swine, how full of cant you are!

Herbert Hensley Henson commented on one of Lang's sermons: 'Lang's oration in Canterbury Cathedral yesterday was, of course, very eloquent, and expressed in terms of sonorous platitude, which could neither wake criticism in the hearers, nor bind obligations on the orator.'

When Henson was Bishop of Durham he went to see Lang, who was then Archbishop of York. When he arrived at Bishopsthorpe he was shown a newly painted portrait of the Archbishop. Lang asked him: 'What do you think of it?'

'What do *you* think of it?' Henson said.

'I don't like it,' the Archbishop replied. 'It makes me too much of the proud, pompous prelate.'

'And which of these adjectives,' Henson answered, 'would you consider inappropriate, Your Grace?'

Another critic was the popular biographer Hesketh Pearson, as described by Richard Ingrams:

> Hesketh Pearson took the War in his stride. His main worry was not Hitler but the Archbishop of Canterbury. On June 17, 1940 he noted:

> 'The Archbishop of Canterbury called the nation to pray yesterday for the French people. The prayer was answered at midnight, when the French army laid down its arms.'

Talking to an old lady in the village of Whatlington, he shocked and surprised her by referring to the Archbishop as Public Enemy No. 1:

> 'I quickly ran over his malign exploits. His national Day of Prayer for Poland was followed by the collapse of Poland. His ditto for France resulted in ditto. And last Sunday's prayers for England have been speedily followed by the signing of a pact between Hitler and Jugoslavia. The man is a menace, and if he proposes another Day of Prayer I hope he'll be put in a padded cell. God obviously dislikes him very much.'[7]

One hopeful incident occurred today; the Archbishop of Canterbury has resigned. This aged prelate has done irreparable damage to the Church of England; narrow, snobbish to a fantastic degree, cold, political, vengeful, he has emptied the churches and alienated thousands of people. He has never been right on any issue, and is hated by Laymen and Ecclesiastics alike. His evil face, thin lips, hard, small, terrible eyes are enough to frighten even an adult. Only his voice redeemed him, and his dignity – though it was the dignity of a Grand Inquisitor. Winston (Churchill) loathed him.

The Diary of Sir Henry ('Chips') Channon, entry for 2 January, 1942

Jan. 20th. Hughie (Kingsmill) came to lunch, and we were much amused by an extract from Archbishop Lang's memoirs in the *Sunday Times*, particularly the statement that on a stalking expedition, in order to protect the King from a heavy shower, 'the Archbishop, claiming the privilege of a subject to cover the person of his Sovereign, lay down on top of him.' On this awesome picture Hughie dwelt at great length, imagining what would have been the

---

reaction of some Highland ghillie who had come upon the monarch and the archbishop thus disposed under an overhanging rock.[8]

Some bishops, like other clergy, have had lapses of memory and moments of absent-mindedness.

Dr Robert Sanderson, a Bishop of Lincoln, had according to John Aubrey 'no great memorie, I am certain not a sure one; when I was a fresh-man and heard him read his first lecture, he was out in the Lord's Prayer . . . Had his memorie been greater his judgement had been less: they are like two well-buckets.'

∾∾∾

Bishop Gilbert Burnet's absence of mind was well known. Once he was having dinner with Sarah, Duchess of Marlborough, after her husband's disgrace. The bishop compared the great victor of Blenheim to Belisarious.

'But,' asked the Duchess, 'how came it that such a man was so miserable, and universally deserted?'

'Oh, madam,' exclaimed the *distrait* prelate, 'he had such a brimstone of a wife!'

∾∾∾

Lord William Cecil, Bishop of Exeter, was also noted for his absent-mindedness. He was once on a train and unable to find his ticket when asked for it.

'It's all right, my Lord,' said the inspector, 'we all know who you are.'

'Yes,' said the bishop, 'but if I can't find my ticket, I don't know where I'm going.'

'Which way was I going?' Lord William once asked an acquaintance when he stopped for a chat. When he was told that he was travelling *away* from the palace, he said, 'Thank you! Then I must have had my breakfast.'

At a dinner the lady on his left was given water. 'Could I have some wine, please?' she asked Cecil.

'My apologies,' he said, 'I thought that you were a member of the Temperance League.'

She replied, 'Oh, no – a member of the Purity League.'

'So sorry,' answered the bishop, 'I knew that there was something that you did not do.'

During a very cold spell, so the story goes, he remarked to a friend: 'My wife's feet are the coldest of any woman I have slept with.'

On one rainy day he was driven into Exeter by car, but returned home on a bicycle that was not his. When he realized his mistake, he rang the police, who told him the name of the owner. He rode back into Exeter at once and propped the bicycle against the side of the house where it belonged. He apologized profusely – and immediately got on it again and pedalled away.

'Burglar Bill', as he was known in the diocese, pedalled away on other men's bicycles so often that eventually the episcopal model was painted bright red. The colour had to be changed to yellow, however, after he arrived home on a postman's bike.

∾∾∾

I am surprised it does not strike the mountaineers how very much the great emoluments of the Church are flung open to the lower ranks of the community. Butchers, bakers, publicans, schoolmasters, are perpetually seeing their children elevated to the mitre. Let a respectable baker drive through the city from the west end of the town, and let him cast an eye on the battlements of Northumberland House, has his little muffin-faced son the smallest chance of getting in among the Percies, enjoying a share of their luxury and splendour, and of chasing the deer with hound and horn upon the Cheviot Hills? But let him drive his alum-steeped loaves a little further, till he reached St. Paul's Churchyard, and all his thoughts are changed when he

sees that beautiful fabric; it is not impossible that his little
penny roll may be introduced into that splendid oven.
Young Crumpet is sent to school – takes to his books –
spends the best years of his life, as all eminent Englishmen
do, in making Latin verses – knows that the *crum* in crumpet
is long, and the *pet* short – goes to the University – gets a
prize for an Essay on the Dispersion of the Jews – takes orders
– becomes a Bishop's chaplain – has a young nobleman for
his pupil – publishes an useless classic, and a serious call
to the unconverted – and then goes through the Elysian
transitions of Prebendary, Dean, Prelate, and the long train
of purple, profit, and power.   Sydney Smith[9]

Jonathan Swift wrote these lines after 'seeing a worthy Prelate go
out of the Church in the Time of Divine Service, to wait on his
Grace the Duke of Dorset':

> Lord Pam in the Church (cou'd you think it) kneeled
>   down,
> When told the Lieutenant was just come to Town,
> His Station despising, unaw'd by the Place,
> He flies from his God, to attend to his Grace;
> To the Court it was fitter to pay his Devotion,
> Since God had no hand in his Lordship's promotion.

And this was his 'Advice to a Parson':

> Wou'd you rise in the Church, be Stupid and Dull,
> Be empty of Learning, of Insolence full,
> Tho' lewd and Immoral, be Formal and Grave,
> In Flatt'ry an Artist, in Fawning a Slave,
> No Merit, no Science, no Virtue is wanting
> In him, that's accomplish'd in Cringing and
>   Canting . . .[10]

Some bishops, following nature rather than grace, were enthusiastic
about looking after their own, and offered advancement and preferment in the Church to their clerical sons and sons-in-law. Bishop

Sparke was the Bishop of Ely from 1812 to 1836. He gave so many of the best livings in his diocese to members of his own family, that it was said locally that you could find your way across the Fens on a dark night by the number of little Sparkes along the road. People quoted the Book of Job in relation to these promotions: 'Man is born to trouble, as the Sparkes fly upward'.

He was the last Bishop of Ely to exercise temporal jurisdiction. When he hanged the leaders of the Littleport Riots his coachman refused to take him to witness the executions. An Act of Parliament followed to remove his jurisdiction.

Vernon Harcourt, Archbishop of York, was in his ninety-second year when he took a walk with his chaplain in October, 1847. They walked across a wooden bridge over an ornamental pool at Bishops-thorpe. The bridge collapsed and they both fell into the water up to their necks. The Archbishop faded away and died a few weeks later. The *Times* obituary slyly implied that his family connexion with powerful politicians had contributed to his own rise to high office. It observed that 'the progress of his professional advancement though perhaps not much beyond his deserts, was at least fully equal to them'.

He himself ordained his own nephew into a family living with no regard for the traditional lapses of time in the Church between one order and the next and the conventional pauses between steps on the ladder of promotion. 'I think it will save both you and me some trouble if I shoot you through both barrels,' he said, 'so I will ordain you both deacon and priest this afternoon.'

It obviously helped to further one's career if one was related to a bishop. It helped even more if one was the son of a cardinal. Cardinal Thomas Wolsey had at least two illegitimate children. He found a place for his daughter at a convent in Shaftesbury. When Thomas, his son, was still at school, Wolsey made him Dean of Wells, Provost of Beverley, Archdeacon of York, Archdeacon of Richmond, Chancellor of Salisbury, Prebendary of Wells, York, Salisbury, Lincoln and Southwell, and Rector of Rudby, Yorkshire and St Matthew's, Ipswich.

❧❧❧

Bishop Pollock, after the Second World War, was largely responsible for the rebuilding of Norwich Cathedral. The dinner to celebrate the restoration work was held on the same day that the bishop's young wife had produced their first child. The bishop, emotionally exhausted, nodded off during a speech. The speaker said: 'And I am sure we would all like to congratulate the Bishop and his wife on their most happy event earlier this day'. All eyes turned to the sleeping bishop. His chaplain hastily shook him and said: 'My Lord, they are congratulating you.' He rapidly rose to his feet and blurted out: 'Please, please, ladies and gentlemen, I assure you, the Dean had quite as much to do with it as I did.'

❧❧❧

Lord Denning told a story about a bishop going to preach at the Temple Church in London, where the lawyers congregate and where the acoustics are not good. The verger said to the bishop: 'Pray, my Lord, speak very clearly and distinctly because the agnostics here are terrible.'

❧❧❧

Hostesses at Edwardian house parties often discreetly made arrangements for their guests to abet their extramarital liaisons. Husbands and wives were sometimes allotted separate rooms to be conveniently nearer their lovers. Ardent Lotharios, however, could make mistakes. One night Lord Charles Beresford crept into what he supposed was the dark bedroom of his mistress. He jumped into the vast bed shouting 'Cock-a-doodle-doo' and found himself on top of the Bishop of Chester and his wife.

❧❧❧

8.45 a.m. morning's post brought me a number of circulars.
From the Bishop of Chelmsford, enclosing a letter from
the two English primates with orders to read it [a Pastoral
Letter calling for continued prayer along with war work] on
Sunday, June 6th. *The Star* (evening newspaper of Wedn. 2
June 1915) commented on this arch-episcopal utterance
with force and humour: 'Gas and Gaiters'.

Andrew Clark, diary entry for 5 June, 1915[11]

∾∾∾

The Bishop's Mistake

The Bishop glanced through his window pane
On a world of sleet, and wind, and rain,
When a dreary figure met his eyes
That made the bishop soliloquize.

And as the bishop gloomily thought
He ordered pen and ink to be brought,
Then 'Providence Watches' he plainly wrote
And pinned the remark to a ten bob note.

Seizing his hat from his lordly rack
And wrapping his cloak around his back,
Across the road the bishop ran
And gave the note to the shabby man.

That afternoon was the bishop's 'at home'
When everyone gathered beneath his dome,
Curate and canon from far and near
Came to partake of the bishop's cheer.

There in the good old bishop's hall
Stood a stranger lean and tall,
'Your winnings, my lord,' he cried. 'Well done –
"Providence Watches", at ten to one.'

It is to be noted on Sunday next
The bishop skilfully chose his text,
And from the pulpit earnestly told
Of the fertile seed that returned tenfold.

Anon.

∾∾∾

A bishop was staying as a guest in a large house. He took a bath and saw a reflection of his stark naked body in a large pier-glass. He expressed his horror and a poet responded to his shock.

Lines To A Bishop Who Was Shocked (A.D. 1950) At Seeing A Pier-Glass In A Bathroom

Beneath that Chasuble, my Lord, that holds
You close (as Charity all men enfolds);
Beneath that Cope that, opening before,
Of Life Eternal signifies the Door,
And (as Durandus taught) recalls the strength
Of godly Perseverance by its length;
Beneath that Rochet of pure lawn, and whiter
Than Iceland's winter cap; beneath that Mitre;
A body stands concealed, which God once chose
The Spirits of his Children to enclose,
And (as a Bishop surely must believe)
His Very Self Incarnate to receive.
Yet, through a mirror suddenly aware
That 'Temples of the Spirit' can be bare,
You shrink aghast, with pained and puzzled eyes,
While God's great laughter peals about the skies.

Sir Lawrence Jones[12]

DEANS

In the Church of England a dean presides over a chapter of canons,
the clergy who run a cathedral. A dean is also administrator of a
collegiate church. The title can be applied to the senior member of
some academic, diplomatic and legal bodies. At Oxford and Cambridge universities the dean is a college fellow with responsibility
for undergraduate discipline. The word comes from the Late Latin
word *decanus*, which signifies one set over ten persons.

There have been several famous deans of cathedrals, including
John Colet, John Donne, Jonathan Swift and W. R. Inge. Colet
founded St Paul's School in London and a preparatory school feeding
that public school is called Colet Court. The production of bio-
graphical and critical studies on Donne and Swift is a major literary
industry. Inge, like Colet and Donne, was the Dean of St Paul's. He
was a man of academic distinction and one of the most brilliant
writers of the twentieth century.

∾∾∾

Dr Price, once the Dean of Hereford Cathedral, is fondly remembered by many only because John Aubrey in his *Brief Lives*
recorded the following anecdote:

> This Deane was a mighty Pontificall proud man and that
> one time when they went in Procession about the Cathedral
> church, he would not doe it the usual way in his surplice,
> hood, etc, on foot, but rode on a mare thus habited, with
> the Common prayer booke, in his hand reading. A stone
> horse [stallion] happened to breake loose, and smelt the
> mare, and ran and leapt her, and held the Reverend Deane
> all the time so hard in his Embraces, that he could not
> gett off till the horse had done his bussinesse. But he would
> never ride in procession afterwards.[13]

A letter to The Times, *30 September 1937*

Sirs,

By the lamented death of the Dean of Westminster a remarkable coincidence and (to an old Trinity man) a proud one, is broken through. Hitherto on his way north, he could have breakfasted with the Dean of Westminster, lunched with the Dean of Peterborough, had tea with the Dean of York, and dined with the Dean of Durham – all members of his college.

The Rectory,   Yours faithfully,
Finchley, N3.[14]   Stewart F. C. Bernays
                                             (Trinity College, Oxford)

∾∾∾

A Rural Dean, or nowadays Area Dean, is a senior clergyman with responsibilities for a subdivision of an archdeaconry, a rural deaconry or deanery. In his poem 'The Old Vicarage Grantchester', Rupert Brooke wrote of the garden of the parsonage of his father:

> Curates, long dust will come and go
> On lissom, clerical, printless toe;
> And oft between the boughs is seen
> The sly shade of a Rural Dean.[15]

Rural or Area Deans combine their responsibilities with their work as parish priests. In 'Lines from a Parish Magazine' a rural dean displays his ability to steer a middle course. The *via media*, halfway between Geneva and Rome, became an Anglican ideal, a mark of moderation and tolerance. At times this is not the best policy. The ideal can also become an excuse for sitting on the fence, a cover-up for indecisive thought and action, as has been indicated in the stance of certain bishops and as can be seen in this poem:

> I am a loyal Anglican
> A Rural Dean and Rector;
> I keep a wife and pony trap,
> I wear a chest protector.

I should not like my name to be
Connected with a party;
But still my type of service is
Extremely bright and hearty.

Of course one has to keep abreast
Of changing times and manners;
A Harvest Festival we keep
With Special Psalms and banners;
A Flower-Service in July,
A Toy-Fund Intercession,
And when the hens lay well, we hope
To start an Egg-Procession.

My wife and I composed a form
For dedicating hassocks,
Which (slightly changed) we also use
For surplices and cassocks;
Our Bishop, when we sent it for
His Lordship's approbation,
Remarked: 'A very primitive
And pleasing compilation.'

To pick the best from every school
The object of my art is,
And steer a middle course between
The two contending parties.
My own opinion would no doubt
Be labelled 'High' by many;
But all know well I could not wish
To give offence to any.

One ought, I'm certain, to produce
By gradual education
A tone of deeper Churchmanship
Throughout the population.
There are, I doubt not, even here
Things to be done in plenty;
But still – you know the ancient saw –
'Festina lenta – lente'.

I humbly feel that my success,
My power of attraction,
Is mainly due to following
This golden rule of action:
'See us from all men's point of view,
Use all men's eyes to see with,
And never preach what anyone
Could ever disagree with.'

G. W. E. Russell[16]

JONATHAN SWIFT

As has been noted, critical studies and biographies of Jonathan Swift
have become a major literary industry. A sparkling biography on
him has been written by Victoria Glendenning, published by Hutchinson in 1998. Swift lived between 1667 and 1745, and in 1726 he
wrote perhaps the greatest satire in the English language – *Gulliver's
Travels*.

The epitaph on Swift's tomb in St Patrick's Cathedral, Dublin
was written by himself:

Hic Depositum Est Corpus
JONATHAN SWIFT, S.T.P.
Huius Ecclesiae Cathedralis
Decani.
Ubi Saeva Indignatio
Ulterius Cor Lacerare Nequit
Abi Viator.
Et Imitare, Si Poteris,
Strenum Pro Virili Liber-
tatis Vindicem.
Obiit Anno MDCCXLV
Mensis Octobris Die 19
Aetatis Anno LXXVIII.

A translation:

> Here lies the body of Jonathan Swift,
> Doctor of Divinity, Dean of this Cathedral
> Church, where savage indignation can no
> longer lacerate his heart. Go, traveller,
> and imitate if you can one who with all his
> might championed liberty.

This is a free version composed by W. B. Yeats:

> Swift has sailed into his rest;
> Savage indignation there
> Cannot lacerate his breast.
> Imitate him if you dare,
> World-besotted traveller; he
> Served human liberty.[17]

> That sovereign mind;
> Those bleak, undaunted eyes;
> Never to life, or love, resigned –
> How strange that he who abhorred cant, humbug, lies,
> Should be aggrieved by such simplicities
> As age, as ordure, and as size.
>
> > Walter de la Mare[18]

The Incomparable Dean

> A man is made of many parts:
> Though women all have tender hearts
> And never bully or betray,
> A man is built another way.
> The warring fires that in him burn
> May show a seeming unconcern,
> But give a limping dog a lift.
> And thus it was with Doctor Swift.

In judgement harsh, in outlook sour,
Disdainful both of wealth and power,
He lashed the follies of mankind,
But oft forgot where last he dined.
He laboured to expose the dense
By pure and simple commonsense,
Pouring the bounty of his wit
On all who stood in need of it.

The world moves on. The wind has changed,
And everything is rearranged;
But generations still prefer
To travel far with Gulliver.
Stella he loved, Vanessa too,
And to a higher love stayed true:
'Fair Liberty' was all his cry;
For her he stood prepared to die.

Roger Woddis[19]

Dean Jonathan Swift on Dean Jonathan Swift

In November, 1731, Swift wrote these lines about his own death. They
were occasioned by his reading the Rochefoucauld maxim: 'In the Ad-
versity of our best friends, we find something that does not displease us.'

'Behold the fatal Day arrive!
How is the Dean? He's just alive.
Now the departing Prayer is read:
He hardly breathes. The Dean is dead.
Before the Passing-Bell begun,
The News thro' half the Town has run.
O, may we all for Death prepare!
What has he left? And who's his Heir?
I know no more than what the News is,
'Tis all bequeath'd to publick Uses.
To public Use! A perfect whim!
What had the Public done for him!
Meer Envy, Avarice, and Pride!

He gave it all: – But first he dy'd.
And had the Dean, in all the Nation,
No worthy Friend, no poor relation?
So ready to do Strangers good,
Forgetting his own Flesh and Blood?' . . .

'Perhaps I may allow; the Dean
Had too much Satyr in his Vein;
And seem'd determin'd not to starve it,
Because no Age could more deserve it.
Yet, Malice never was his Aim;
He lash'd the Vice, but spar'd the Name.

No individual could resent,
Where Thousands equally were meant.
His satyr points at no Defect,
But what all Mortals may correct:
For he abhorr'd that senseless Tribe,
Who call it Humour when they jibe:
He spar'd a Hump, or crooked Nose,
Whose Owners set not up for Beaux.
True genuine Dullness mov'd his Pity,
Unless it offer'd to be witty.
Those, who their Ignorance confess'd,
He ne'er offended with a Jest;
But laugh'd to hear an Idiot quote,
A Verse from *Horace*, learn'd by Rote.'

'He knew an hundred pleasant Stories,
With all the Turns of *Whigs* and *Tories*:
Was chearful to his dying Day,
And Friends would let him have his Way.
He gave the little Wealth he had,
To build a House for fools and Mad:
And shew'd by one satyric Touch,
No Nation wanted it so much' . . .[20]

Quotations from Jonathan Swift

A man should never be ashamed to own he has been in the wrong, which is but saying, in other words, that he is wiser today than he was yesterday.

And he gave it as his opinion, that whoever could make two ears of corn or two blades of grass to grow upon a spot of ground where only one grew before, would deserve better of mankind, and do more essential service to his country than the whole race of politicians put together.

There's none so blind as they that won't see.

We have just enough religion to make us hate, but not enough to make us love one another.

If Heaven had looked upon riches to be a valuable thing, it would not have given them to such a scoundrel.

The stoical scheme of supplying our wants by lopping off our desires is like cutting off our feet when we want shoes.

Promises and pie-crusts are made to be broken.

ARCHDEACONS

Archdeacons in the Church of England are administrative assistants to bishops. They are like an adjutant in the army. In a given area (an archdeaconry) they are involved in the placement and induction of priests to new parishes, in the examination of those about to become priests, in the discipline of the clergy, and in church build-ings and finances. They are available to give advice about practical ecclesiastical matters. Until the second half of the twentieth century they customarily wore gaiters.

> There was an Archdeacon who said:
> 'May I take off my gaiters in bed?'

> But the Bishop said: 'No,
> Wherever you go
> You must wear them until you are dead.'

Anon.

> If your church roof's leakin'
> Or your hall floor's creakin'
> Or your Warden's not speakin'
> Or your Curate is cheekin'
> Or your Bishop's no beacon
> Before you weaken
> Consult the Archdeacon.

Anon.

Geoffrey Chaucer indicated their considerable power in the twelfth century:

> . . . And ere the bishop caught them with his crook
> They were all down in the Archdeacon's book,
> And he has jurisdiction, on inspection,
> And powers to administer correction.

In the twelfth century one Archdeacon of York was clearly envious of the power of an Archbishop of York, William Fitzherbert. When Fitzherbert first came to York in procession with the clergy, the wooden bridge carrying him over the Ouse collapsed. No one perished then, but he did not last long: the malicious Archdeacon, serving at a mass at which the Archbishop was celebrating, finished him off by slipping poison into the communion wine.

Chaucer also, with tongue in cheek, described the duties of archdeacons:

> In my own district once there used to be
> A fine archdeacon, one of high degree,
> Who boldly did the execution due
> On fornication and on witchcraft too,

Bawdry, adultery and defamation,
Breaches of wills and contract, spoliation
Of church endowment, failure in the rents
And tithes and disregard of sacraments,
All these and many other kinds of crime
That need have no rehearsal at this time,
Usury, simony too. But he could boast
That lechery was what he punished most.

from *The Friar's Tale*[21]

Dr Grantley is a great comic figure in the 'Chronicles of Barsetshire' series of novels by Anthony Trollope. He was the Archdeacon of Barchester. Trollope wrote of him:

> We believe, as a general rule, that either a bishop or his archdeacons have sinecures. Where a bishop works, archdeacons have but little to do, and *vice versa*. In the diocese of Barchester the Archdeacon did the work. In that capacity he was diligent, authoritative, and, as his friends particularly boasted, judicious. His great fault was an overbearing assurance of the virtue and claims of his order, and his great foible an equally strong confidence in the dignity of his own manner and the eloquence of his own words. He was a moral man, believing the precepts which he taught, and believing also that he acted up to them; though we cannot say that he would give his coat to the man who took his cloak, or that he was prepared to forgive his brother even seven times.[22]

Criticisms of archdeacons have been amusingly fiercer than those of Trollope. John of Salisbury was a learned scholar. He was a friend of Thomas Becket and eventually became Bishop of Chartres. In about 1160 he wrote that from archdeacons 'the whole way of salvation is utterly barred', because 'they love gifts, they follow rewards, they give a prize to injustice, they rejoice in false accusations, they feed upon the sins of the people'.

When Gilbert of Sempringham, who died in 1189, was approached by Alexander, Bishop of Lincoln, to be an archdeacon, he declined, saying, 'that he knew not a shorter way to perdition'.

William Doune, an Archdeacon of Leicester, died in 1361 with much on his conscience. He expressed repentance for all the extortions he had made or that had been made on his behalf, and in his will he ordered restitution to be made. He provided the medieval age with a rare sight: a contrite and humble archdeacon.

VICARS

As a parish priest a vicar now has exactly the same status as a rector. Time was when a priest, appointed by a bishop to have the cure of souls in a parish, was always a rector or 'ruler'. When a parish was in the care of a monastery, the abbot would appoint a vicar, from the Latin *vicarius*, a 'substitute', to perform the parochial duties. The rector had the right to the tithes of a parish. He would sometimes appoint a vicar to read the services vicariously in his place. The absenteeism of rectors sometimes became notorious. Some rectors became wealthy with a plurality of parishes at the expense of poverty-stricken assistant clergy or curates.

A book that reflects the large place played by vicars in English social life is *The Parson in English Literature*, edited by F. E. Christmas, published by Hodder and Stoughton in 1950. Curiously it makes no mention of one of the greatest of English comic novels – *The Vicar of Wakefield* by Oliver Goldsmith. The Barchester novels of Anthony Trollope about clerics are a national treasure. In more recent times the continuous amusement afforded by vicars has been evidenced in the television series *The Vicar of Dibley*.

In the Foreword of *The Anglican Parochial Clergy: A Celebration* by Michael Hinton,[23] the author wrote:

> Melancholy the task of surveying the parochial clergy of the Church of England may in some respects be; but there is also much to lift the heart. 'Celebration' is the right word.

We do well to keep these words in mind when reading anecdotes and verses about vicars which tend to dwell on their frailties.

> The fact that Hawker kept nine or ten cats which followed him to church and careered around it during the service time; that Francis Pickford, the aged rector of Hagworth-ingham, tamed squirrels during the eighteen-eighties; that Edward Long of White Roothing was fond of kissing little girls; and that Samuel Parr used to smoke his pipe in the vestry and sometimes during intervals in the service itself, would as like as not, be the kind of traits to endear rather than repel.
>
> A. Tindall Hart[24]

> As a body of men, parsons have been so put upon, so much the butt of humour and derision, so often warmly loved and warmly hated, that it is difficult to paint them in unexaggerated colours. We laugh at the parson but he is not contemptible; we protest when his authority rises too high or when his weakness trips him up, but he exists both as a leader and a fellow sufferer at our own invitation; he comes unfitted for the task and yet we bow to his experience.
>
> Simon Goodenough[25]

During a service news was brought to the vicar of the Cornish village of Poughill of a shipwreck. There were often rich pickings to be taken from such calamities. The priest walked down the nave as far as the font in his surplice. He then flung off his ecclesiastical garb and shouted: 'My Christian brethren, there's a ship wrecked in the cove; let us all start fair.'

ಎಎಎ

A broad-minded vicar was asked by a progressive headmistress to talk to the older girls in her school about Christianity and sex. The vicar's wife was more prudish and less tolerant so he told her that he was going to give the girls a talk about sailing.

Later in the week the headmistress met the vicar's wife in the street and said to her: 'Your husband was so good to talk to my girls the other evening – he was so helpful and informative.'

'I can't imagine what he knows about it,' replied the vicar's wife, 'he's only done it twice, and the first time he was sick and the second time his hat blew off.'

∾∾∾

A vicar informed his verger that he had lost his bike. He declared that on the following Sunday he would, during his sermon, slowly and deliberately read out the Ten Commandments and would pause significantly when he came to 'Thou shalt not steal.' It was then up to the verger to study the faces of the congregation and try to pick out the culprit.

During the sermon the vicar did read through the Commandments, but did so without a significant pause. The verger asked him after the service why he did not pause. 'When I got to "Thou shalt not commit adultery,"' the vicar replied, 'I remembered where I had left my bike.'

∾∾∾

'Come on, Robin. Finish your breakfast or you will be late for church.'

'I don't want to go to church,' said Robin.

'But you must,' said his mother.

'The Sunday School teachers hate me.'

'Even so . . .'

'The children too – they all hate me as well.'

'I am sorry but you still have to go.'

'But why must I?' wailed Robin.

'Well,' said his mother, 'for one thing you are fifty-five years old, and, for another thing, you are the vicar.'

∾∾∾

A vicar was calling around his parish. He knocked at the door of one house several times, but got no answer in spite of the fact that a neighbour assured him that someone was in. He left his visiting card, writing on it: 'Revelation 3:20: Behold I stand at the door and knock; if anyone hears my voice and opens the door I will come to him.'

On the next Sunday a woman attended a church service and gave the vicar her card. It was inscribed: 'Genesis 3:10.' He later looked it up and read: 'I heard the sound of thee in the garden and I was afraid, because I was naked and hid myself.'

Blame the Vicar

When things go wrong it's rather tame
To find we are ourselves to blame,
It gets the trouble over quicker
To go and blame things on the vicar.
The vicar, after all, is paid
To keep us bright and undismayed.
The Vicar is more virtuous too
Than lay folks such as me and you.
He never swears, he never drinks,
He never *should* say what he thinks.
His collar is the wrong way round,
And that is why he's simply bound
To be the sort of person who
Has nothing very much to do
But take the blame for what goes wrong
And sing in tune at Evensong.
For what's a Vicar really for
Except to cheer us up? What's more,
He shouldn't ever, ever tell
If there is such a place as Hell,
For if there is it's certain he
Will go to it as well as we.
The Vicar should be all pretence
And never, never give offence.
To preach on Sunday is his task
And lend his mower when we ask

And organize our village fetes
And sing at Christmas with the waits
And in his car to give us lifts
And when we quarrel, heal the rifts.
To keep his family alive
He should industriously strive
In that enormous house he gets,
And he should always pay his debts,
For he has quite six pounds a week,
And when we're rude he should be meek
And always turn the other cheek.
He should be neat and nicely dressed
With polished shoes and trousers pressed,
For we look up to him as higher
Than anyone, except the Squire.
Dear People, who have read so far,
I know how really kind you are,
I hope that you are always seeing
Your Vicar as a human being,
Making allowances when he
Does things with which you don't agree.
But there are lots of people who
Are not so kind to him as you.
So in conclusion you shall hear
About a parish somewhat near,
Perhaps your own or maybe not,
And of the Vicars that it got.
One parson came and people said,
'Alas! Our former Vicar's dead!
And this new man is far more "Low"
Than dear old Reverend so-and-so,
And far too earnest in his preaching,
We do not really like his teaching,
He seems to think we're simply fools
Who've never been to Sunday Schools.'
The Vicar left, and by and by
A new one came, 'He's much too "High",'

The people said, 'too like a saint,
His incense makes our Mavis faint.'
So now he's left and they're alone
Without a Vicar of their own.
The living's been amalgamated
With one next door they've always hated.

John Betjeman[26]

The Vicar of Bray

Simon Aleyn was the Vicar of Bray in Berkshire from 1540 to 1588, during the four reigns of Henry VIII, Edward VI, Mary and Elizabeth. He was a Roman Catholic, then a Protestant, then a Catholic again and, finally, a Protestant once more. When he was accused of being a turncoat, he answered: 'Not so for I always keep my principle, which is this, to live and die the Vicar of Bray.'

As a result, long before the Civil War there was a Berkshire proverb: 'The Vicar of Bray will be Vicar of Bray still.' The song about the Vicar of Bray was written, however, with reference to Dr Francis Carswell, who was at Bray from 1667 to 1709. In it the vicar claims to have been a High Church man under Charles II, a Catholic under James II, a Protestant under William, a Tory under Anne and a Whig under George I. The last claim in fact could not be true because Francis Carswell no longer held the living by the time George I was King of England.

These verses were written anonymously:

In good King Charles's golden days,
    When loyalty no harm meant,
A zealous high-church man was I
    And so I gained preferment.
Unto my flock I daily preached,
    Kings are by God appointed,
And damned are those who dare resist,
    Or touch the Lord's anointed.
And this is law, I will maintain
    Until my dying day, sir,

That whatsoever king shall reign,
  Still I'll be Vicar of Bray, sir!

When royal James possessed the crown,
  And Popery grew in fashion;
The penal laws I hooted down,
  And read the Declaration:
The Church of Rome I found would fit
  Full well my constitution,
And I had been a Jesuit,
  But for the Revolution.
And this is law, etc.

When William was our king declared,
  To ease the nation's grievance,
With his new wind about I steer'd,
  And swore to him allegiance:
Old principles I did revoke,
  Set conscience at a distance,
Passive obedience is a joke,
  A jest is non-resistance.
And this is law, etc.

When Royal Anne became our queen,
  The Church of England's glory,
Another face of things was seen,
  And I became a Tory:
Occasional Conformists base,
  I blamed their moderation,
And thought the Church in danger was,
  From such prevarication.
And this is law, etc.

When George in pudding-time came o'er,
  And moderate men looked big, sir,
My principles I changed once more,
  And so became a Whig, sir:
And thus preferment I procured,
  From our faith's great defender,

And almost every day abjured
>The Pope and the Pretender.
And this is law, etc.

The illustrious House of Hanover,
>And Protestant Succession,
To these I lustily will swear,
>Whilst they can keep possession:
For in my faith and loyalty,
>I never more will falter,
But George my lawful king shall be –
>Until the times do alter.
And this is law, I will maintain
>Until my dying day, sir,
That whatsoever king shall reign,
>Still I'll be Vicar of Bray, sir!

The following verses about an automatic vicar were first published in 1957. Since then the technological terms have changed, but the gist is clear. The significance of '1928' is that in that year the Church of England produced a new Prayer Book. It was rejected by Parliament, but generally welcomed by broad or moderate churchmen. A 'spike' is a High churchman. Those who think that bishops are the *esse* of the church suppose that they are essential for the existence of the Church.

Automation

Our automatic Vicar is the very latest thing,
A fine precision instrument, to pray and preach and
>sing;
He thunders in the pulpit and sparkles at the font,
And serves the congregation with precisely what they
>want.

Deriving automation from a neat atomic pile,
He's easily adjusted on a calibrated dial;
Agreeing with his Council whatsoever they dictate
When fed with resolutions on a perforated plate.

By quite an elementary adjustment of a wire,
He's high or low or moderate, whichever we require;
And since his teaching modulates by turning on a knob,
In matters ecumenical he's really just the job.

The Bishop is delighted that his operative rate
Is permanently stabilized at 1928;
Diocesan officialdom appreciates him most,
For here is a phenomenon who answers all his post.

We've had a long succession of eccentrics and of spikes,
But now we have a clergyman whom everybody likes;
And all await the future of mechanical research,
When automatic bishops are the *esse* of the Church.

S. J. Forest[27]

The following poem celebrates the parson-poet Robert Herrick (1591–
1674). His ministry was exercised, from 1629 until his death, in the
small parish of Dean Prior, five miles from Totnes. There, besides
writing his verses, he delighted in reviving old country customs: the
Christmas hollying, wassailing, and mumming; Twelfth Night feasts,
maypoles, St John's Midsummer Fires, and Harvest Homes.

On the Reverend Herrick

Rare old Herrick, the Cavalier Vicar
Of pleasant Dean Prior by Totnes town,
Rather too wont of foaming liquor
The care of these troublous times to drown.
Of wicked wit by no means chary,
Of ruddy lips not at all afraid,
If you gave him milk in the Devonshire dairy
He'd probably kiss the dairy maid . . .
Lover of ruby and amber wine,
Of joyous humour and charming girls,
Hater of cant about things divine,
Of hypocrite Cromwell, and all his churls.

Mortimer Collins[28]

A Hand in the Bird

I'm a maiden who is forty,
And a maiden I shall stay.
There are some who call me haughty,
But I care not what they say.

I was running the tombola
At our church bazaar today,
And doing it with gusto
In my usual jolly way . . .

When suddenly, I knew not why,
There came a funny feeling
Of something *crawling up my thigh*!
I nearly hit the ceiling!

A mouse! I thought. How foul! How mean!
How exquisitely tickly!
Quite soon I know I'm going to scream.
I've got to catch it quickly.

I made a grab. I caught the mouse,
Now right inside my knickers.
A mouse my foot! It was a HAND!
Great Scot! It was the vicar's!

                              Roald Dahl[29]

There was a young lady of Tottenham,
Who'd no manners, or else she'd forgotten 'em;
    At tea at the vicar's
    She tore off her knickers
Because, she explained, she felt 'ot in 'em.

                              Anon.

CURATES

In medieval Latin *cura* meant spiritual oversight. The curate was thus the priest with the 'cure' or care of the souls in a parish. The word is used in this sense in *The Book of Common Prayer*: 'Give grace, O heavenly Father, to all Bishops and Curates . . .'

The word acquired a more limited meaning, that of the clergyman who assisted a rector or vicar. He often came to be seen as impoverished and down-trodden, as Jonathan Swift and Sydney Smith depicted him.

The curate has also been a figure of gentle ridicule and bachelor curates have frequently attracted the devotion of the unmarried ladies of the parish. This was illustrated on an early twentieth-century comic card with the caption:

Vicar: I've been looking for a Curate for over twelve months!
Lady: That's nothing! I've been looking for one for over twelve years!

∾∾∾

In a Victorian book called *Our Mothers* there was an illustration entitled 'The New Curate'. A very proper young man is sitting nervously on the edge of a chair, top hat on the floor beside him. He sips his tea under the critical gaze of two formidable matrons. Their daughters eye him with interest. The caption reads:

Eager curiosity over the new curate is inevitable among the softer sex. He will certainly be their associate, if at all an eligible gentleman, in charitable organisations as well as lawn tennis and croquet; possibly he may become someone's life partner.

∾∾∾

In a *Punch* cartoon of November 1895 a wretched curate was addressed by his bishop: 'I'm afraid you've got a bad egg, Mr Jones!'
He answered: 'Oh no, my Lord, I assure you! Parts of it are excellent!'

The curate's half-rotten egg, accepted with pathetic politeness, became the symbol of the curate's lot. It also came to mean anything that was bad but could euphemistically be described as only partly so.

∾∾∾

When Mervyn Hayt was Bishop of Coventry he invited Cosmo Lang, Archbishop of Canterbury, to a luncheon party. Amongst the guests was a bashful curate, who, in his confusion, suggested to the Archbishop: 'Have another piece of Grace, your Cake.'

∾∾∾

The young curate, fresh from college, arrived in the village where he was to take up his first appointment, on a Saturday afternoon. A football match between the local team and one from an adjoining parish was taking place. Reporting to the Rectory, and finding that he was free until the next morning, when he would be required to officiate at Matins, he decided to go and watch the game. Being a football enthusiast, he made the most of the occasion, and joined in the cheering and shouting, loudly, with the rest of the onlookers. The result was that he found that he had almost lost his voice at the end of the game.

Fearing that he might not recover his voice by the morning, he made his way back to the Rectory, with the idea of asking to be excused from duty on Sunday. The door was answered by the Rector's pretty daughter, to whom he had already been introduced, and in a stage whisper he enquired if her father was in.

'No,' she whispered back, seizing him by the hand, 'We're quite safe for at least an hour – so come in.'

∾∾∾

Like so many vicars, he had a poor opinion of curates.
P. G. Woodhouse in *Mr. Mulliner Speaking*

∾∾∾

Jonathan Swift constructed two different styles of clerical living in
'The Parson's Case'. In the first state, as a curate, a man may reasonably want to commit suicide; but in the second he would surely
want to live as long as he could.

> That you, friend Marcus, like a stoick
> Can wish to die, in strain heroick,
> No real fortitude implies:
> Yet, all must own, thy wish is wise.
> Thy curate's place, thy fruitful wife,
> Thy busy drudging scene of life,
> Thy insolent illit'rate vicar,
> Thy want of all-consoling liquor,
> Thy thread-bare gown, thy cassock rent,
> Thy credit sunk, thy money spent,
> Thy week made up of fasting days,
> Thy grate unconscious of a blaze,
> And, to compleat thy other curses,
> The quarterly demands of nurses,
> Are ills you wisely wish to leave,
> And fly for refuge to the grave:
> And, O what virtue you express
> In wishing such afflictions less!
> But, now shou'd fortune shift the scene,
> And make thy curate-ship, a dean;
> Or some rich benefice provide,
> To pamper luxury and pride;
> With labour small, and income great;
> With chariot less for use than state;
> With swelling scarf, and glossy gown,
> And license to reside in town;
> To shine, whereall the gay resort,
> At concert, coffee house, or court;
> And weekly persecute his grace
> With visits, or to beg a place;
> With underlings thy flock to teach,
> With no desire to pray or preach;

With haughty spouse in vesture fine,
With plenteous meals, and gen'rous wine;
Woud'st thou not wish, in so much ease,
Thy years as num'rous as thy days?[30]

The Reverend Sydney Smith defended a curate against a bishop in *The Edinburgh Review* in 1822.

A Curate – there is something which excites compassion in the very name of a Curate! How any man of Purple, Palaces, and Preferment, can let himself loose against a poor working man of God, we are at a loss to conceive, – a learned man in an hovel, with sermons and saucepans, lexicons and bacon, Hebrew books and ragged children – good and patient – a comforter and a preacher – the first and purest pauper in the hamlet, and yet showing, that, in the midst of his worldly misery, he has the heart of a gentleman, and the spirit of a Christian, and the kindness of a pastor; and this man, though he has exercised the duties of a clergyman for twenty years – though he has most ample testimonies of conduct from clergymen and respectable as any Bishop – though an Archbishop add his name to the list of witnesses, is not good enough for Bishop Marsh; but is pushed out in the street, with his wife and children, and his little furniture, to surrender his honour, his faith, his conscience and his learning – or to starve![31]

The Dean of — deserves to be preached to death by wild curates.   Sydney Smith[32]

The essayist G. W. E. Russell related how Lady Comtermere, an octogenarian dame, kindly invited a young curate whom she had been asked to befriend to take part in a 'spelling-bee'. He got on splendidly for a while, and then broke down among the repeated 'n's' in 'drunkenness'. Returning crestfallen to his suburban parish, he was soon horified to hear the rumour that he had been turned out of a lady's house in the West End for drunken-ness.

∾∾∾

A curate had worked hard on a speech for a public meeting. When he arrived he was told that he was only required to lead the gathering in prayer. Determined not to waste his material, he therefore embodied his speech in his prayer, one passage of which went: 'Lest this point be too obscure, O Lord, permit Thy servant to illustrate it with an anecdote . . .'

∾∾∾

A timid bachelor curate and a beautiful young girl were madly in love, and they were strolling round the churchyard in the evening and sat for a rest on a large tombstone.

'I thought we might discuss the hereafter,' said the curate nervously.

'That's original,' said the girl. 'But if you're not hereafter what I'm hereafter, you'll be hereafter I've gone.'

∾∾∾

A curate was about to give his first sermon in a village and the vicar asked him what his text would be. The curate said: 'The widow's mite.' The vicar observed: 'There are only two widows in the village and they both do.'

∾∾∾

An angry young curate of Kent
Commanded his flock to repent;
        But they, full of ire
        At his threat of hell-fire,
Told him where to go; so he went.

L. Ashton

An Anglican curate in want
Of a second-hand portable font
   Will exchange for the same
   A photo (with frame)
Of the Bishop-Elect of Vermont.
Ronald Knox

CLERGY WIVES

A remark often made by Roman Catholic priests to the priests of the Church of England, comparing their own presbyteries and celibate state with Anglican vicarages and freedom of priests to marry, is: 'We have better quarters, but you have better halves.' The wives of some clergy have indeed been the strength and stay of their husbands and the life and soul of many parishes. Nevertheless they have not always been an unmixed blessing.

From the first, Queen Elizabeth I was unhappy with married bishops. This is reflected in perhaps the most celebrated anecdote about wives of the clergy. After having had lunch with Archbishop Matthew Parker at Lambeth Palace, she said to Mrs Parker: 'Madam I may not call you; mistress I am ashamed to call you. So I know not what to call you; but I thank you.'

∾∾∾

There was a widely circulated story that in the early nineteenth century on the list of suitable candidates for ecclesiastical promotion at Lambeth Palace, the mysterious letters 'W.H.M.' and 'W.I.' would appear by certain names. They stood for 'Wife Has Means' and 'Wife Impossible'.

E. L. Hicks, Bishop of Lincoln, known in clerical circles as Bumbo, had such an impossible wife that she was known in the diocese as 'The Lincoln Handicap'.

∾∾∾

'Who is it,' a bishop is reputed to have asked a page boy, 'that sees and hears all we do, and before whom even I am but a crushed worm?'

The boy answered: 'The Missus, My Lord.'

❧❧❧

In the past bishops often continued in office when they were certainly and certifiably demented. Others in their households, according to Sydney Smith, tended to take over their episcopal responsibilities. He wrote with some comic exaggeration: 'I have seen in the course of my life, as the mind of the prelate decayed, wife bishops, daughter bishops, butler bishops, even cook and housekeeper bishops.'[33]

❧❧❧

Certainly the most celebrated bishop's wife in fiction was Mrs Proudie. This is how Anthony Trollope described the bishop's reaction to her death:

> She had in some ways, and at certain periods of his life, been very good to him. She had kept his money for him and made things go straight, when they had been poor. His interests had always been her interests. Without her he would never have been a bishop. So, at least, he told himself now, and so told himself probably with truth. She had been very careful of his children. She had never been idle. She had never been fond of pleasure. She had neglected no acknowledged duty. He did not doubt that she was now on her way to heaven. He took his hands down from his head, and clasping them together, said a little prayer. It may be doubted whether he quite knew what he was praying. The idea of praying for her soul, now that she was dead, would have scandalized him. He was certainly not praying for his own soul. I think he was praying that God might save him from being glad that his wife was dead.[34]

One clergyman seems to have been excessively humble and grateful in relation to his wife's acceptance of him. The lady went by the name of Greenwood. Her husband wrote these memorable lines on her epitaph:

> Her graces and her qualities were such
> That she might have married a bishop or judge;
> But so extreme was her condescension and humility
> That she married *me*, a poor doctor of divinity;
> By which heroic deed, she stands confest,
> Of all other women, the phoenix of her sex.

∾∾∾

A certain dean was extraordinarily proud of his wife when she not only had a book published, but also produced a son. To congratulate him on his son and heir, a friend said, 'Congratulations, Mr Dean.'

The Dean answered, 'Yes, I consider it a very estimable performance on the part of my wife considering that I gave her no assistance, and she had very little help from the minor canon.'

∾∾∾

Another remarkable woman was the wife of another dean, Dr Overall of St Paul's. John Aubrey described him as:

> . . . most remarqueable by his Wife, who was the greatest
> Beautie of her time in England. That she was so, I have it
> attested from the famous Limmer Mr Hoskins, and other
> old Painters, besides old Courtiers. She was not more
> beautifull than she was obligeing and kind and was so
> tender-hearted that (truly) she could scarce denie any one.
> She had (they told me) the loveliest Eies that were ever
> seen, but wondrous wanton. When she came to Court, or
> to the Play-house, the Gallants would so flock about her,
> Richard the Earle of Dorset, and his brother Edward, since
> Earle, did mightily adore her. And by their report he must

have had a hard heart that did not admire her. Bishop
Hall sayeth in his Meditations that there is none so old,
that a beautiful person loves not, nor so young, whom a
lovely feature moves not.

The good old Deane, notwithstanding he knew well that
he was horned, loved her infinitely: in so much that he
was willing she should enjoy what she had a mind to.

Among others who were charmed by her was Sir John
Selby, of Yorkshire. Old Mrs Tyndale (who knew her)
remembres a song made of her and Sir John, part whereof
was this, viz:

> The Deane of Paule's did search for his wife,
>   and where d'ee thinke he found her?
> Even upon Sir John Selbye's bed,
>   as flatte as any Flounder.[35]

7 *In the Study*

SCHOLARS

Time was when a clergyman was expected to spend his mornings reading and writing in his study. Some country parsons had ample leisure to pursue their varied scholarly interests in divinity, history, science, horticulture, everything and anything. The English countryside has the finest natural history thanks to the dedicated labours of clergymen like Gilbert White (1720–93), the author of *The Natural History of Selborne*. An examination of the achievements of such men has been made by Patrick Armstrong in *The English Parson – Naturalist*, subtitled 'A Companionship Between Science and Religion'.[1]

The scholarship of clergymen was not confined to rural retreats. Oxford and Cambridge Universities were once clerical institutions. Certain ecclesiastical positions, like the Deaneries of St Paul's and Westminster Abbey in London, were often filled by learned and talented men. One biographer wrote:

> The members of the Church of England have been reputed,
> of all others, the slackest to celebrate their own worthies,
> partly, I conceive, from the humility and modesty of their
> principles and education, partly from the great multitude
> of incomparable scholars therein to be commemorated,
> that such labours would be almost infinite.

Here we will not enter into such endless labour, but highlight some amusing aspects of such scholars and note when they themselves were amusing.

∽∾∽

Henry Carrington is one of many examples that could be offered of a versatile parson-scholar, whose range of interests, both academic and athletic, were an adornment to his parish. Critics of the exercise of such multifarious activities by a priest should note the faithfulness of his service to his parish. In 1904 it was written of him:

> The Very Reverend Henry Carrington is approaching his sixtieth year of his term of office as dean and rector of Bocking, Braintree. The son of Sir Edmund Carrington, first Chief Justice of Ceylon, he was born in the year before Waterloo. Educated at Charterhouse and Caius College he entered the Church in 1838 as curate of Hadleigh in Suffolk, but he has been in Essex since 1839. He has translated Victor Hugo, Thomas à Kempis, and Baudelaire, and has published an anthology of French poetry. He has stated that his recreations are 'geology, Greek, chess, landscape gardening, formerly fencing, skating, lawn tennis and sketching'. Probably it is his many occupations which have given him such a long lease of life.[2]

DIVINITY

Since the union of divinity and humanity is the great article of our religion, it is odd to see some clergymen in their writings of divinity wholly devoid of humanity.

Jonathan Swift

Thinkers of the world should by rights be guardians of the world's mirth.

Agnes Repplier

It is laughable that Christian theologians, who ought to make love paramount, have been notorious for their *odium theologicum*, their malice that torments each other.

> So oft in theologic wars
> The disputants, I wean,

Rail on in utter ignorance
Of what each other mean.

Anon.

A theological student named Fiddle
Refused to accept his degree.
'It is bad enough to be Fiddle,' he said,
'without being Fiddle D.D.'

∾∾∾

The solemn study of divinity can always verge on absurdity. The
nineteenth-century poet Coventry Patmore made this point in his
couplet:

Shall I, a gnat which dances in Thy ray,
Dare to be reverent?

We are never more ridiculous than when we are being pompous
and our pomposity is at its most absurd when we solemnly pontifi-
cate about the mind of God. God knows how some divines have
thought they know exactly what God knows. One theologian
declared that so great is the presumption of writing about God that
he could only hope that, 'in addition to an inexhaustible depth of
mercy and kindness the divine heart possesses an irrepressible sense
of humour'.

The following lines were written after the heresy trial of Bishop John
Colenso of Natal, who had been urged to resign by Charles Longley,
Archbishop of Canterbury.

The Archbishop:

My dear Colenso, with regret,
We hierarchs in conclave met,
Beg you, you most disturbing writer,
To take off your colonial mitre;
This course we urge upon you strongly:
Believe me, yours most truly, LONGLEY.

The Bishop:

> My dear Archbishop, to resign
> This Zulu diocese of mine,
> And own myself a heathen dark,
> Because I've doubts of Noah's Ark,
> And think it right to tell men so –
> Is *not* the course for, COLENSO.
>
>   Anon.

                    ∾∾∾

These verses were written about four heretics whose views about the humanity and divinity of Jesus were condemned by theologians regarded as orthodox.

> There once was a parson called Arius,
> Whose doctrinal errors were various;
>   Of demeanour ascetic,
>   But opinions heretic,
> The Logos he made secundarius.

> A classical man, Apollinarius,
> Revived some of the tenets of Arius;
>   In Laodicea
>   He had the idea
> There could not be two persons contrarious.

> Like the cunning old man of Baucalis,
> He denied an anima rationalis;
>   There could only be sarx,
>   And then – question marks –
> Perhaps anima animalis.

> The Bishop of Byzant, Nestorius,
> In a heresy truly notorious,
>   Held a whole human nature
>   And denied Dei Mater;
> But Cyril at length proved victorious.

An error by Leo extinguished,
Which Eutyches should have relinquished,
    By dogmatic profusion
    Created confusion
Of the natures which should be distinguished.

So here's to these heretics four,
Though to learn their ideas is a bore;
    And the wretched sub-tutor
    If he'd been acuter,
Would have thought of this method before.

Anon.

In nineteenth-century Oxford there lived a fat Doctor of Divinity and his equally corpulent physician brother. This anonymous lampoon was written about them:

Here D.D. toddles, M.D. rolls,
Were ever such a brace of noddies?
D.D. has the cure of souls,
M.D. has the cure of bodies.

Between them both what treatment rare
Our bodies and our souls endure;
One has the cure without the care,
And one the care without the cure.

❧❧❧

'Sicut in Caelo, et in Terra'*

When members of our Island Race
Are domiciled in Outer Space,
Let no one fear that they will be
Neglected by the C. of E.
The Bench of Bishops will (I feel)

---

* 'On earth as it is in heaven'

Be prompt to issue an Appeal
For funds to purchase and equip
An evangelic Rocket-Ship.
The Diocese of Mars and Moon
Will thus be born, and very soon
May flit across the Stellar scene
The sly shade of a Lunar Dean.
Yet even here, alas, will come
Dark theologic odium,
And practices irregular
Dismay Ebor and Cantuar
For complex is the cure of souls
Remote from earth's magnetic poles.
(Just how, on Pluto, can a priest
Be sure that he is facing East?)
And since the planets never run
Isochronously around the sun,
Anomalies must soon appear
In the Ecclesiastic Year.
The Feast of Magnus Martyr, say,
Might be a Martian Ember Day,
Or Saturn's Advent coincide
With Neptune's Lent or Lammas-tide.
Enormous difficulties, too,
Await hymnologists – for who
Could bid his 'earth-bound soul arise'
While soaring through the farther skies?
Such are the problems that will face
The theologian in Space;
Beside the Athanasian Creed
They'll seem the merest chicken-feed.

E. V. Milner[3]

Screams, A & M

At the time that the Beatles first became popular I. T. Ramsey, a
brilliant theologian who became Bishop of Durham but died tragic-

ally young, made the following plea for a theological understanding
of modern culture:

> Here was a cosmic disclosure – Beatle language was virtu-
> ally theological language. If we wish to coin a revelant
> theology, it is our duty to learn, not scoff.

A poet wrote this somewhat cynical riposte:

> Hark, the Herald Angels scream,
> Letting off their holy steam,
> And with glad, hysteric cries
> Loud Thy screaming Church replies.
>
> Free from sorrow, free from sense,
> Free from mere intelligence,
> Free from boring questions of
> Faith and works and hope and love,
>
> Vice and virtue melt away
> 'neath our mystic manic bray –
> Who could ponder heaven or hell,
> Deafened by our endless yell?
>
> Quadripartite deity,
> May we have the luck to be
> Thy most fortunate of saints
> Who, replete with screaming, faints.
>
> Four in One and One in Four,
> May we scream for evermore
> Round Thy nickel-plated throne,
> Groan and scream and scream and groan.
>
> And through all eternity
> May Professor Ramsey be
> Set by Thee in glory there,
> Not to scream, but just to hear.
>
> Peter Dickinson[4]

RICHARD PORSON

Richard Porson (1759–1808) was widely regarded as the greatest Greek scholar that England had ever produced. He was nicknamed 'The Great Grecian'. Educated at Eton College and Trinity College, Cambridge, he became the Regius Professor of Greek at Cambridge and was buried in the chapel of Trinity College.

He smoked and drank excessively and when he became heated in argument with a refractory opponent he would occasionally use a poker to reinforce his point of view. He was shunned by all except those who found his wit and scholarship irresistible. Servants sometimes found him smoking in the common room in the morning without apparently having moved from the place where he had been left overnight.

He had notoriously high animal spirits. He was said once, for a wager, to have carried a young lady round the room in his teeth.

He sometimes put the Greek Folio of Galen, the physician, under his pillow at night; this was not, as he used to observe, because he expected medicinal virtue from it, but because his head had to be kept high in order to relieve his asthma.

On a Fellow of Trinity College Porson wrote:

> Here lies a Doctor of Divinity;
> He was a Fellow too of Trinity.
> He knew as much about Divinity,
> As other Fellows do of Trinity.

Remarks attributed to Richard Porson

He once returned to his rooms to discover that his gyp or college servant had failed to put out his candle and toddy, which he took every night. He looked and looked for them until he finally sighed: 'oudé tode (pronounced 'toddy') oudé t'allo (pronounced 'tallow')', meaning 'neither one thing nor another'.

He was at a dinner party when the conversation turned to Captain Cook and his famous voyage. Someone anxious to join in asked Porson: 'Pray, was Cook killed on his first voyage?'

'I believe he was,' said Porson, 'though he did not mind it much and immediately set sail for his second voyage.'

'Life', he once remarked, 'is too short to learn German.'

After a dispute someone said to him: 'Dr Porson, my opinion of you is most contemptible.'

'Sir,' answered Porson, 'I never knew an opinion of yours that was not contemptible.'

A very junior scholar once rashly suggested to Porson that they should collaborate in a book. The professor commented: 'Put in all I know and all you don't know and it will be a great work!'

He conveyed to Robert Southey his opinion of Southey's poems: 'I will tell you, Sir, what I think of your poetical works; they will be read when Shakespeare's and Milton's are forgotten –' then after a pause – 'but not till then.'

HENRY GEORGE LIDDELL

Henry George Liddell (1811–98) is included here not because of his own wit, but because of a witty verse about him and an ironic aspect of his life.

Liddell's name is inextricably linked with that of Robert Scott. They were both born in 1811 and both placed in the First Class in the Oxford list of 1833. They were both Doctors of Divinity and in 1843 the Greek–English Lexicon of Liddell and Scott was published. In the following 150 years it passed through nine editions and made their names celebrated in the realm of classical studies.

Liddell's name is also linked with that of another Anglican clergyman, Thomas Teasdale. He was the curate of Luckington in Wiltshire and for ten years laboured at producing a Greek dictionary. Pipped at the post by Liddell and Scott, he is a largely forgotten figure, whilst they achieved huge scholastic fame. This is one of the saddest tales in the history of English publishing.

When Edward, the Prince of Wales, went up to Christ Church, Oxford in 1881, Liddell was made his director of studies. It must have been an uphill struggle. Queen Victoria wanted to reward him with the offer of the Deanery of Westminster Abbey, but he declined.

'The Broad' and 'The High' are the names of the two main streets of Oxford. 'Broad' and 'High' also denote different brands of church-manship in the Church of England. Cecil Spring-Rice, the author of the hymn 'I vow to thee my country', wrote these lines on Liddell:

> I am the Dean of Christ Church, Sir,
> This is my wife – look well at her.
> She is the Broad; I am the High:
> We are the University.

Another version of the first two lines goes:

> I am the Dean, and this is Mrs Liddell:
> She plays the first, and I the second fiddle.

Such is the irony of fame that Liddell's worldwide celebrity came to rest more on the fathering of his ten children than on his massively erudite work. One of the children was Alice, the inspiration of Lewis Carroll's *Alice in Wonderland*.

BENJAMIN JOWETT

Benjamin Jowett was born on 15 April, 1817, and died, unmarried, on 1 October, 1893. The 'Jowler' was an outstanding figure in his time. For twenty-eight years he was a tutor at Balliol College, Oxford, and for twenty-three he was the Master of Balliol. He was a classical scholar and a translator of Plato.

Nevertheless his main life-work lay with pupils and friends at Balliol and Oxford, where he became Vice-Chancellor in 1882. He was largely responsible for making Balliol a nursery of remarkable public men: proconsuls, statesmen, diplomats, lawyers, historians, philosophers, and poets.

He was keen that people should develop and use their talent, and he did not like incompetence. He was not, however, as arrogant as this celebrated and anonymous verse suggests:

> First come I; my name is Jowett.
> There's no knowledge, but I know it.
> I am the Master of this College.
> What I don't know, isn't knowledge.

Remarks attributed to Benjamin Jowett

A young atheist in Balliol College is said to have told him: 'I cannot see any signs of God in nature, and when I look into my own heart I cannot find him there.'

Jowett commanded: 'You must either find him by tomorrow morning or leave the college.'

'Do you really think, Master,' he was once asked, 'that the Stoics or Epicureans were right in saying that a good man might be happy on a rack?'

'Well,' Jowett replied, 'perhaps a very good man on a very bad rack.'

One undergraduate declared to him that it was his ideal to dedicate his life to the pursuit of Truth. Jowett commented: 'You can get up to £900 a year for that, but no more than that.'

To an undergraduate who said that he was devoting his life to a search for the Holy Grail, he asked: 'And what will you do with the Holy Grail when you find it, Mr Bowen?'

Of another undergraduate he commented: 'The time that he can spare from the adornment of his person he devotes to the neglect of his duties.'

Even the youngest amongst us is not infallible.

Give the clergy your sympathy; don't give them anything else.

It is most important in this world to be pushing, it is fatal
to seem so.

WILLIAM ARCHIBALD SPOONER

William Archibald Spooner was born in 1844 and died in 1930. He
was Warden of New College, Oxford, from 1903 to 1924, and his
biographer Sir William Hayter points out that there are not many
like him in our history. By giving us those felicitously transposed
phrases known as 'spoonerisms' he belongs to that select company
whose surnames have added words to the English language: sandwich, mackintosh, wellington, cardigan, boycott, lynch, bowldlerize,
macadam.

It is claimed that while Spooner was Warden New College's reputation as a happy place continued to grow. C. M. Bowra said that
there was something saintly about him, and Julian Huxley also used
the word 'saintly' when recalling the Warden and his college.

A modest and tolerant man, he wrote of himself in his diary:
'Every now and then a great yearning to be clever and famous comes
over me, but I know in my heart that I have not got it in me . . . I
shall never be more than I am – a moderately useful man.' His
qualities are illustrated by the fact that during the First World War
he insisted on posting the names of Germans killed, who had been
at New College, on the Chapel door. When the war was over their
names were also included on a memorial tablet together with all the
other old members of the college who had fallen.

It is difficult to be certain how many so-called spoonerisms can
actually be attributed to him. There is no doubt that he sometimes
fell into metaphrasis – the technical name for the transposition of
sounds. He suffered from a mild cerebral dysfunction which led him
to transpose words and ideas. Nevertheless he was able to exploit,
and even create, a confusion to get out of a difficulty. Sometimes,
after speaking, he would add: 'Oh dear; have I said *one of those
things?*'

Spoonerisms

Lord David Cecil claimed that the only spoonerism genuinely produced by Spooner occurred just after the First World War. He was
looking out of the window in the Warden's lodgings and saw an
undergraduate in the quad whose face was familiar. He went down
and said to him: 'Now tell me, was it you or your brother who was
killed in the war?'

He is reported to have said: 'I remember your name perfectly, but
I just can't think of your face.'

Spooner is said to have said to Stanley Casson, just after he had
become a don at the college: 'Do come to dinner tonight to meet
our new fellow, Casson.'
    'But Warden, I *am* Casson.'
    The Warden replied: 'Never mind, come all the same.'

∾∾∾

It has been noted that we cannot be sure how many spoonerisms
were really his. Many of them must have been the products of lively
undergraduate minds.

To a delinquent undergraduate: 'You have deliberately tasted two
worms. You have hissed my mystery lessons. You were fighting a lion
in the quadrangle. You will have to leave Oxford by the town drain.'

Passing a widow dressed in mourning clothes, he confided to his
companion: 'Poor soul! Very sad! Her late husband, you know – a
very sad death – eaten by missionaries – poor soul!'

In a sermon he referred to 'seeing in a dark, glassly'.

In another: 'Which of us has not felt a half-warmed fish?'

To an optician: 'Have you a signifying glass?'
    'A *what*, sir?'
    'Oh, it doesn't magnify.'

On seeing a cat fall from a window: 'It popped on its little drawers.'

Announcing a hymn: 'Kinkering kongs their tatles tike' – for 'Conquering kings their titles take'.

'Is the bean dizzy?' – for 'Is the dean busy?'

'Let us drink to the queer old dean' – for 'Let us drink to the dear old queen.'

'Will nobody pat my hiccup?' – for 'Will nobody pick my hat up?'

An old lady supposedly caught the habit from him, and, when she found someone sitting in her favourite pew, complained: 'Someone is occupewing my pie.'

Dr Spooner answered: 'I am very sorry, madam; I'll sew you another sheet.'

'From Land's End to John of Gaunt.'

'He's out at the back – boiling his icicle.'

On one occasion Spooner had to give two sermons on the same day. In the morning he was at Winchester College, and in the afternoon he was to address the massed Mothers' Unions of Hampshire. At one stage during his morning sermon he solemnly told the young Wykehamist scholars: 'All of you have hands horny with toil, and many of you are mothers.'

'You will find as you grow older that the weight of rages will press harder and harder on the employer.'

WILLIAM RALPH INGE

William Ralph Inge (1860–1954) was said to be the most famous ecclesiastic, and one of the most famous writers, of his time. He had a rare combination of brains and personality. He is included here not only because he prompted witty verses about him, but also because he often expressed his own wisdom wittily.[5]

George Bernard Shaw saw that he was 'our most extraordinary churchman, our most extraordinary writer, and in some vital respects our most extraordinary man'. He was the only man before whose intellect Shaw bowed. Shaw wrote what he called 'An Ingenious Rhyme on the Gloomy Dean':

> If you his temper would unhinge
> And his most sacred rights infringe,
> Or, excommunicated, singe
> Where friends forever writhe and cringe
> Imploring that a drop of ginge-
> Rale may on their tongues impinge,
>   Address him then as Doctor Inge;
>
> But if you prize the proper thing
> Be sure to call him Doctor Ing,
> (Unless, your ignorance to screen,
> You temporize with Master Dean),
> But be advised by me and cling
> to the example of the King
>   And fearlessly pronounce him Ing.
> Then rush to hear him have his fling
> In Paul's and places where they sing.[6]

There was a half-truth embedded in his famous nickname, 'The Gloomy Dean'. He fought against any naive belief in the progress of man. He once remarked: ' "You forget," said the Devil with a chuckle, "that I have been evolving too." ' Nevertheless he also claimed that no Christian could be a pessimist because Christianity was a system of radical optimism.

∾∾∾

The following verses were composed about him:

> Hark the herald angels sing
> timidly, because Dean Inge
> has arrived, and seems to be
> bored with immortality.
>   Humbert Wolfe[7]

'The Gloomy Dean' they call our Inge,
But he is really no such thing.
For, though I never heard him preach,
I've known him make a funny speech.

Owen Seaman[8]

Surely for him among the Saints
Will be a special niche
Who had the courage to espouse
The causes of the rich.

An anonymously suggested
epitaph for Dean Inge

∾∾∾

One of the most celebrated comments about him was a sly dig at
his journalistic activities. He was described as 'a pillar of the Church
and two columns of the *Evening Standard*'.

∾∾∾

George Bernard Shaw, whose respect for Inge has already been noted,
wrote a glowing tribute to him in the form of a book review:

> In reading a book for review it is convenient to mark the
> passages which call for comment, and note the numbers
> of the pages. This book [Inge's Second Series of *Outspoken
> Essays*] contains 275 pages. The number of passages which
> call for notes of pure admiration is considerably more than
> 275 ... the book is review proof. The man with enough
> faculty and knowledge for it – and he would be a rare bird
> indeed – would not have the space for it ... One can only
> say again that here is a mind so splendidly efficient, and a
> character so gentle and noble, that the otherwise somewhat
> deplorable aspect of the Church of England is transfigured
> by the strange accident that their possessor is Dean of St.
> Paul's.[9]

Quotations from W. R. Inge

I have never understood why it was considered derogatory to the Creator to suppose that he has a sense of humour.

A man may build himself a throne of bayonets but he cannot sit on it.

When our first parents were driven out of Paradise, Adam is believed to have remarked to Eve: 'My dear, we live in an age of transition.'

It is becoming impossible for those who mix with their fellow men to believe that the grace of God is distributed denominationally.

I am afraid that the clergyman's God is too often the head of the clerical profession.

I had a passage of arms with Miss Ruth Fry, the Quaker. She wanted to show 'infinite Christian love' towards the Bolsheviks, which is like stroking a tiger on the head and calling him 'Poor Puss'.

It is useless for the sheep to pass resolutions in favour of vegetarianism while the wolf remains of a different opinion.

If you marry the Spirit of your own generation you will be a widow in the next.

Worry is the interest paid on trouble before it is due.

Originality, I fear, is too often only undetected and frequently unconscious plagiarism.

Always give the public exactly what they want and ten per cent more than they expect.

Literature flourishes best when it is half a trade and half an art.

> We thought that lines were straight and Euclid true;
> God said, 'Let Einstein be', and all's askew.

The object of studying philosophy is to know one's own mind, not other people's.

Religion is caught, not taught.

The nations which have put mankind most in their debt have been small states – Israel, Athens, Florence, Elizabethan England.

During the 1914–18 war we said we were fighting to make the world safe for democracy. That was a huge lump of sugar for the American eagle, and fortunately for us, he swallowed it.

It may be doubted whether nature intended the Englishman to be a money-making animal.

In dealing with Englishmen you can be sure of one thing only, that the logical solution will not be adopted.

Don't fancy yourself disinterested when you are only uninterested, and don't fancy yourself attracted to God when you are only repelled by man.

Events in the past may be roughly divided into those which probably never happened and those which do not matter.

The Baron de Cambronne did not say at Waterloo, 'The Guard dies, but does not surrender.' Cambronne himself, twenty years later, disavowed the saying, and added with great honesty, 'In the first place, we did not die, and in the second place, we did surrender.'

Independence is no passport to success in a world where, as Swift said, climbing and crawling are performed in much the same attitude.

∾∾∾

When he arrived in New York, a reporter asked him: 'Well, Dr Inge, what do you think about prohibition?'

'I am quite prepared to stick it for three weeks,' he said, 'but, since you ask me, I think cold water, with which the Psalmist says wild asses quench their thirst, is a poor beverage to offer a human being.'

He was questioned by another reporter about what he thought of the morals of the modern 'flapper' as compared with those of her grandmother. He answered: 'The early indiscretions of the flapper's grandmother I neither witnessed nor shared.'

During a period of constant industrial unrest, he commented: 'The working man is sawing at the branch on which he is seated.'

In his *Outspoken Essays* he described public opinion as 'a vulgar, impertinent, anonymous tyrant who deliberately makes it unpleasant for anyone who is not content to be the average man'.

RONALD KNOX

Ronald Knox (1888–1957) was one of the four sons of a Bishop of Manchester.[10] An obituary described him as 'the wittiest churchman in England since Sydney Smith; he was as earnest as he was witty and devout as he was diverting'.

He was first ordained as an Anglican priest and later became a Roman Catholic priest. He was a prolific author, including works of Christian apologetics and polemics, satires and detective stories. His two greatest academic achievements, however, were his translation of the Vulgate edition of the Bible and his study of seventeenth- and eighteenth-century ecclesiastical history, *Enthusiasm: A Chapter in the History of Religion*.

Whilst he was still an undergraduate his devastating wit was heard at an Oxford Union Debate when he said: 'The honourable gentlemen have turned their backs on their country and they now have the effrontery to say that they have their country behind them.'

When someone pronounced, 'The only aspirated S in the English language is in the word sugar,' Knox said, 'Are you sure?'

∽∽∽

Several intellectual limericks were attributed to him. The first two go together and are concerned with the problem of perception.

> There was a young man who said, 'God
> Must think it exceedingly odd
>   If he finds that this tree
>   Continues to be
> When there's no one about in the quad.'

'Dear Sir, your astonishment's odd,
I am always about in the Quad.
          And that's why the tree
          Will continue to be
Since observed by, Yours faithfully, God.'

A third took the form of a collect and parodied a type of agnostic Christianity:

O God, for as much as without Thee,
We are not able to doubt Thee,
          Grant us the grace
          To tell the whole race
We know nothing whatever about Thee.

Another was about determinism:

There was a young man who said: 'Damn!
I have suddenly found that I am
          A creature that moves
          On predestinate grooves,
Not a bus, as one hoped, but a tram.'

8 *At Table*

THE BOTTLE

No longer drink only water, but take a little wine for the sake of your stomach and your frequent ailments.

1 Timothy 5:23, NRSV

Wine is God's greatest gift to mankind.   Plato

Burgundy, so fine and delicate, is certainly man's greatest tribute to God.

Maurice des Ombiaux

We should thank God for beer and Burgundy by not drinking too much of them.

G. K. Chesterton

> Hermit hoar, in solemn call,
>   Wearing out life's evening gray;
> Smite thy bosom, sage, and tell,
>   What is bliss, and which the way?
> Thus I spoke; and speaking sigh'd;
>   – Scarce repressed the starting tear; –
> When the smiling sage reply'd –
>   – Come, my lad, and drink some beer.

Samuel Johnson

Beer is proof that God loves us and wants us to be happy.

Benjamin Franklin

It ought to give pause to the most fanatical teetotaller that the only humans worth saving in the Flood were a family of vintners.   Bernard Rudofsky

The religious system that produced Green Chartreuse can never really die.   'Saki' (H. H. Munro)

When the clergyman's daughter drinks nothing but water, she's certain to finish on gin.   Rudyard Kipling

> God made man, frail as a bubble.
> Man made love – love made trouble.
> God made the vine.
> Then is it a sin
> That man made wine
> To drown trouble in?
>
>   Anon.

∾∾∾

In the latter part of his life the novelist Graham Greene enjoyed leisurely lunches with his favourite priest, Father Leopoldo Duran, a Spanish Professor of Literature. They would drink between them three bottles of wine: 'One for the Father, one for the Son and one for the Holy Ghost'.

∾∾∾

There is a strong connection between the brewing of beer and the Church. It was monks who first brewed beer at Burton-on-Trent. In many parishes there were Church Houses, where church ales were sold and where parishioners met for festivities. The connection is still reflected in the names of ales: Abbot's, The Reverend James, Marston's Merrie Monk, Gibb's Bishop's Tipple and Shepherd Neames' Bishop's Finger.

∾∾∾

Church Ales were once a way of raising money for the parish and perhaps were merrier than Jumble Sales and Bazaars. They were not approved by everyone. In 1585 a disapproving and anonymous critic wrote:

> In certain towns, where dronken Bacchus bearies swaie . . . the church-wardens of every parishe, with the consent of the whole parishe, provide halfe a score of twentie quarters of maulte, whereof some they buy of the church stocke, and some is given to them of the parishioners themselves, every one conferring somewhat, according to his abilitie; which maulte being made into very strong ale or beer, is settle to sale, either in the church or some other place, assigned to this purpose. Then when this is set abroache, well is he that can gete the soonest to it, and spend the most at it . . . The money, they say, is to repair their churches and chappels with, to buy bookes for service, cuppes for the celebration of the Sacrament, Surplesses for Sir John, and such other necessaries.

ოოო

Ale, however, has had at least one episcopal blessing. The following lines come from a poem, 'Jolly Good Ale and Olde', by the aptly named John Still (1543–1608), Bishop of Bath and Wells.

> I cannot eate but littyl meate,
> My stomach is not goode
> But sure I thinke that I can drinke
> With him that wears a hood.
> Though I go bare, take ye no care,
> I nothing am a-cold;
> I stuff my skin so full within
> Of jolly good ale and olde.
> Back and side go bare, go bare
> Both foot and hand go cold;
> But, belly, God send thee goode ale enough,
> Whether it be new or olde.

❧❧❧

Alexander Nowell, who lived from about 1507 to 1602, was the Dean of St Paul's Cathedral in London. He is reported to have invented bottled beer.

❧❧❧

Towards the end of the eighteenth century the curate of St Mary's Church, Lastingham, in North Yorkshire, was also the landlord of The Blacksmith's Arms in the village. The Archbishop of York complained about him keeping an inn. The curate answered: 'Your Grace, my stipend is but £30 yearly and my children will go hungry without the inn. Give me £20 more and I will eschew the inn and my children bless you.'

Desmond Seward in *Monks and Wine*, published by Mitchell Beazley, described how the Christian monks of Europe, amidst the general destruction of culture in the Dark Ages, continually improved viticulture. They preserved the knowledge of wine developed by the Romans. Wine was needed for the celebration of the Holy Communion or Mass.

The Benedictines paved the way, but they were closely followed by the Cistercians and Carthusians. Jesuit and Franciscan missionaries later brought wine production to the New World.

In the twelfth century the Black Monks of Battle Abbey were allowed a gallon of wine a day.

It is said that there was a monk, aged 96, at Eitelsbach, who died of *ullage*, a loss of liquid, when his daily allowance was reduced to one litre.

❧❧❧

Nicholas Breakspear is the only Englishman to have become Pope. He was born at Kings Langley in Hertfordshire and was elected as

Adrian IV in 1154. His death came by choking on a fly as he was drinking.

∾∾∾

It was a French Catholic priest, Canon Kir, who had the excellent idea of mixing cassis with white wine or champagne. The drink is now named after him.

∾∾∾

Cardinal Bernis, the confessor of Madame de Pompadour, used to celebrate Holy Communion with a choice Meursault. He said that he would not wish to confront his Saviour with a grimace caused by some foul vintage.

∾∾∾

When Bishop Fugger travelled to Rome in 1111, he sent his servant ahead to mark with 'Est!' ('This is it') the doors of those inns where they sold good wine. At Montefiascone the wine was so good that 'Est! Est!! Est!!!' was chalked on the door. Wine from that place and with that label is still produced today. John Evelyn discovered the wine in the seventeenth century:

> After seven miles riding (passing through a certaine Wood heretofore sacred to Juno) we came to Mount Fiascone, the head of Falisci, a famous people of old tyme, and heretofore Falernum, as renown'd for the excellent Wine, as now for the story of the Dutch Bishop, who lyes buried in Favionos Church with this Epitaph:
>> Propter Est, Est dominus meus mortuus est:
>> because he had drunk too much of the Wine; for it seemes he had commanded his Servant, to ride before, and (enquiring where the best liquor was), to write Est upon the Vessells.
>
> *The Diary of John Evelyn,* 4 November, 1644

∾∾∾

A Swiss clergyman, travelling to England late in the eighteenth century, was shocked to find a room in a tavern in Oxford full of clergymen, 'all with their gowns and bands on, sitting round a table, each with his pot of beer before him'. He wrote:

> They amused themselves by teasing each other with quotations from the Bible until the party was broken up after midnight, by one of them starting up and shouting: 'Damn me, I must read prayers this morning at All Souls.'

∾∾∾

The Reverend James Woodforde not only enjoyed drinking a bottle of port, he also did his own brewing.

> Brewed a vessell of strong Beer today. My two large Piggs, by drinking some Beer grounds taking out of one of my Barrels today, got so amazingly drunk by it, that they were not able to stand and appeared like dead things almost, and so remained all night from dinner time today. I never saw Piggs so drunk in my life, I slit their ears for them without feeling.   James Woodforde, diary entry for 15 April, 1778[1]

> My 2 Piggs are still unable to walk yet, but they are better than they were yesterday. They tumble about the yard and can by no means stand at all steady yet. In the afternoon my 2 Piggs were tolerably sober.   Ibid., 16 April, 1778

> I thank God, had a very tolerable good Night last Night. I drank but very little Wine Yesterday or to day only 2. or 3. Glasses. I used myself before and all last Winter to near a Pint of Port Wine every Day and I now believe did me much harm.   Ibid., 3 August, 1790

Mr. Thorne came to see Nancy this morning. He strongly recommends Port Wine and to drink rather More than less. She drank today between a Pint and a Quart without having the least effect upon the Brain. She has not drank less than a Pint for many Days. Ibid., 29 March, 1797

Nancy was James Woodforde's niece and she lived with him for twenty-four years until his death. She survived him by thirty-eight years – and she also obviously survived that massive port-drinking remedy.

∾∾∾

Smugglers, it seems, found that clergymen were ready customers, for their liquid goods in particular and especially brandy. Rudyard Kipling's 'Smuggler's Song' has these lines:

> Five and twenty ponies,
> Trotting through the dark –
> Brandy for the Parson,
> 'Baccy for the Clerk . . .

On 29 December, 1786, the Reverend James Woodforde received a mysterious consignment of gin and brandy, evidently delivered by smugglers:

> Had another Tub of Gin and another of the best Coniac Brandy brought me this Evening abt 9. We heard a thump at the Front Door about that time, but did not know what it was, till I went out and found the 2 Tubs – but nobody there.

Charles Burton, who was for sixty years the Rector of Lydd on Romney Marsh, was himself an energetic smuggler. He received casks of brandy that were offloaded at Dungeness Point and brought by horse to be stored beneath the tiered seats on either side of his church's nave.

One Sunday morning, just before the service, one of these hidden casks split open and the smell of liquor filled the church. A quick-witted churchwarden, clearly a collaborator of the rector, pretended to faint and was hastily revived by a colleague with so much brandy that the people were put off detecting the original source of the fragrance.

∾∾∾

A reported exchange between a bishop and a parson in eighteenth-century England goes:

Bishop: I have heard that you are drunk.

Parson: I am never drunk on duty, my Lord.

Bishop: When is a clergyman not on duty?

Parson: When he is drunk, my Lord.

∾∾∾

The Reverend William Cole (1714–82), a philosopher and antiquarian, had no difficulty, with a small group of parson friends, in getting through twelve bottles of wine at a sitting: 'More than any Company I ever entertained before,' noted Cole.[2]

Parson Moreton, who became parson of Willenhall in Staffordshire in 1796, could reputedly drink three bottles of wine with his meal.

> In a silent, decent, clerical manner, they toasted Mr. Arabin
> with bumpers of claret.   Anthony Trollope[3]

Lord Sandwich, the alleged inventor of the sandwich and member of the notorious Hell-Fire Club, is said to have told the following anecdote:

> I was in a company where there were ten parsons, and I made a wager privately – and won it – that among them there was not one prayer book. I offered to lay another wager, that among the ten parsons there were half a score of corkscrews – it was accepted; the butler received his

instructions, proceeded to break his corkscrew, and requested any gentleman to lend him one, when each priest pulled a corkscrew from his pocket.

A Dean of Windsor, Gregory Haschard, was an enthusiastic member of another disreputable club, the Order of Little Bedlam. It met at Burghley House under the aegis of the Fifth Earl of Exeter (1686–1749). Between 1694 and 1695 the Dean was painted by Antonio Verrio on the wall of the Fourth George Room, where he is seen as the god Bacchus, half-naked and imbibing immoderately.

Robert Barclay Fox (1817–55) made this diary entry on 7 July, 1833:

> Took some luncheon at Mitchell. After resting an hour there we walked on to Lower St. Columb where we dined on a rasher of bacon and some bread. An original old man was there with whom we were much amused. He told John Richards he was a drunken Farmer. John Richards asked him if his health did not suffer by it? No, he was as healthy as any man in the parish. If his affairs weren't the worse for it? No, he always struck a better bargain drunk than sober. If his conscience did not prick him for it? Not in the least. If the Parson didn't scold him for it? Parson – law, bless your heart the parson ha' got drunk with me scores of times. Thus beaten on every point John Richards was obliged to sound a retreat.[4]

∾∾∾

Interviews between Frederick Temple, Archbishop of Canterbury, and those who were about to be ordained by him were often feared. Temple said to one ordinand on such an occasion: 'I will lie on the couch, as if I were ill. Go out, come in again and "SICK VISIT" me.'

The young man went out, entered the room again, walked up to the Lord Archbishop of Canterbury, looked at him solemnly, wagged his finger and said: 'Freddie, you're on the drink again!'

∾∾∾

Raymond Asquith, in a letter dated 3 November, 1903, described how he witnessed two intoxicated bishops playing cards.

> I was up till four this morning watching Stepney and Cantuar – both drunk – trying to cheat one another at poker; it was a very even match: for tho' Stepney was far more cunning, Cantuar was far less drunk. Such is All Souls Day.

∾∾∾

His noggin fill'd three parts of gin,
Tom puts but little water in,
And blamed for this, the drunken lout
Answers you thus, with looks devout:
'St. Paul (and you'll allow him merit)
Expressly says – "Quench not the Spirit!"'

Anon.

A bumper of good liquor
Will end a contest quicker
Than justice, judge or vicar.

Richard Brinsley Sheridan

The wine they drink in Paradise
They make in Haute Lorraine;
God brought it burning from the sod
To be a sign and signal rod
That they who drink the blood of God
Shall never thirst again.

The wine they praise in Paradise
They make in Ponterey,
The purple wine of Paradise,
But we have at the price;
It's wine they praise in Paradise,
It's cider that they pray.

G. K. Chesterton[5]

A Landlord's Epitaph

Beneath this stone in hope of Zion
Doth lie the landlord of The Lion;
Resigned unto the heavenly Will,
His son keeps up the business still.

When this too too solid flesh shall melt away and I am
called before my Heavenly Father I shall say to him, 'Sire,
I don't remember the name of the village and I don't
remember the name of the girl, but the wine was Cham-
bertin.'   Hilaire Belloc, at the end of an after-dinner speech

FOOD FROM HEAVEN

Yet he commanded the skies above,
        and opened the doors of heaven;
he rained down on them manna to eat,
        and gave them the grain of heaven.
Mortals ate of the bread of angels;
        he sent them food in abundance.
                        Psalm 78:23–25, NRSV

The Reverend James Woodforde was fond of recording in his diary
what he had eaten and drunk. On 27 July, 1774, he wrote about a
dinner and supper that he gave for five guests at New College,
Oxford:

We were very merry and pushed the Bottle on very briskly.
I gave my Company for dinner, some green Pea Soup, a
chine of Mutton, some New College Puddings, a goose,
some Peas and a Codlin Tart with Cream. Madeira and
Port Wine to drink after and at dinner some strong Beer,
Cyder, Ale and small Beer . . . I had a handsome dish of

fruit after dinner ... I gave my company only for supper cold mutton. After supper I gave them to drink some Arrac Punch with Jellies in it and some Port wine. I made all my Company but Dr. West quite merry. We drank 8 bottles of Port one Bottle of Madeira besides Arrac Punch, Beer and Cyder. I carried of my drinking exceedingly well indeed.

Of a later occasion (6 March, 1795) he wrote:

We gave them for Dinner a Couple of boiled Chicken and Pigs face, very good Peas Soup, a boiled Rump of Beef very fine, a prodigious fine, large and very fat Cock-Turkey rosted, Maccaroni, Batter Custard Pudding with Jelly, Apple Fritters, Tarts and Raspberry Puffs. Desert, baked Apples, nice Nonpareils, brandy Cherries and Filberts. Wines, Port and Sherries, Malt Liquors, Strong Beer, bottled Porter, etc. After Coffee and Tea we got to cards ...

∾∾∾

Talking of Pleasure, this moment I was writing with one hand, and the other holding to my mouth a Nectarine – good God how fine. It went down soft, pulpy, slushy, oozy – all its delicious enbonpoint melted down my throat like a large Beatified strawberry.

John Keats to Charles Wentworth Dilke

Writing about his recovery after a serious accident, the doctor and author Oliver Sacks recalled:

I ordered almost everything on the menu – from anchovy toast to rum-balls and meringues – and everything was marvellous, the very food of love (oral music). Not only marvellous, but holy – I felt the meal as a sacrament, my first communion with the world. I had been starved of the world, now, for more than six weeks. With every sacred mouthful – and I ate slowly, though hugely, with thanksgiving and reverence – I felt I was partaking of that holy feast, the world. The substance, the sensuousness, was spiritual as well. The food and drink were blessed – a sacramental feast.[6]

In an otherwise silent religious community, on Easter Day one of the monks was allowed to say a single sentence. The year came round for Brother Martin's turn. He said: 'This porridge is too lumpy.' And then the whole community spent the rest of the year in silence.

The following Easter it was the turn of Brother Andrew. 'The porridge is too runny,' he said. Another whole year went by.

It was time for Brother Hugh to speak. He announced: 'I am leaving the monastery.' The abbot called him to an interview and asked him why he wanted to leave. Brother Hugh answered: 'It's all this *constant* bickering about porridge.'

∾∾∾

Father Healy (on whom see p. 29) once said: 'Lunch is a poor compliment to breakfast and an insult to dinner.'

> The Lord alloweth us sauce with our meat, and recreation with our vocation.
>   Thomas Fuller

> Of all the gifts of God, by far
> the best is Russian caviare.
>   Hilaire Belloc[7]

> Oysters are more beautiful than any religion ... There's nothing in Christianity or Buddhism that quite matches the sympathetic unselfishness of an oyster.
>   'Saki' (H. H. Munro)

The Reverend Morgan Jones (1781–1824) of Blewly, near Didcot in Oxfordshire, was extremely miserly and left a fortune. His sermons were written on scraps of paper. He always wore the same hat and

coat. When his clothes needed to be repaired he removed rags from
scarecrows to patch them. He saved money on food by inventively
and inevitably dining at the expense of others.

∾∾∾

In 1464 a feast for some 600 guests was held when George Neville
was installed as Archbishop of York. Part of the menu included 300
quarters of wheat, 300 tuns of ale, 100 tuns of wine, 1 'pipe of
hippocras' (a large cask of spiced wine), 104 oxen, 6 wild bulls, 1000
sheep, 304 calves, 304 'porkes', 400 swans, 2000 geese, 1000 capons,
2000 pigs, 104 peacocks, besides over 13,500 birds, large and small,
of various kinds. In addition there were stags, bucks, and roes, five
hundred and more, 1500 hot pasties of venison, 608 pikes and
breams, 12 porpoises and seals, besides 13,000 dishes of jelly, cold
baked tarts, hot and cold custards, and 'spices, sugared delicates,
and wafers plentie'.

Sydney Smith made fun of the Archbishop of Canterbury's extrava-
gant and grand entertaining:

> Is it necessary that the Archbishop of Canterbury should
> give feasts to Aristocratic London; and that the domestics
> of the Prelacy should stand with swords and bag-wigs
> round pig, and turkey, and venison, to defend, as it were,
> the Orthodox gastronome from the fierce Unitarian, the
> fell Baptist, and all the famished children of Dissent?

∾∾∾

> Cooking is one of those arts which most require to be
> done by persons of a religious nature.
>
> Alfred North Whitehead

The worst sailor on board was generally consigned to cook in the
galley of eighteenth-century ships. This explains the proverb used
by English sailors: 'God sends meat, and the Devil sends cooks.'

Ah! We may talk sentiment as much as we like, but the stomach is the real seat of happiness in this world. The kitchen is the chief temple wherein we worship, its roaring fire is our vestal flame, and the cook is our great high-priest. He is a mighty magician and a kindly one. He soothes away all sorrow and care. He drives forth all enmity, gladdens all love. Our God is great, and the cook is his prophet. Let us drink, and be merry.

Jerome K. Jerome[8]

Lord of Creation, may my every guest
By all my kitchen skill be much impressed.
I know you were content with loaves and fishes,
But these days they expect less homely dishes.
May they not spot the traps I've set for mice,
But be beguiled by scents of bread and spice;
Let meals run smoothly from the rough terrine
To summer pudding with sauce mousseline.
Also please, Lord, let them never guess
It's mostly been acquired at M and S.

Lindsay Staniforth[9]

Dean Jonathan Swift supposedly wrote these lines while he was having a breakfast of bacon and eggs at an Irish monastery on a Friday, when the monks were eating fish:

Does any man of common sense
Think ham and eggs give God offence?
Or that a herring has a charm
The Almighty's anger to disarm?
Wrapped in his majesty divine,
D'you think he cares on what we dine?

ოოო

For some years, the Reverend Sydney Smith was in a remote country parish. He wrote of it: 'My living in Yorkshire was so far out of the way that it was actually twelve miles from a lemon.' He once described his friend Henry Luttrell's idea of heaven as 'eating paté de foie gras to the sound of trumpets'.

These are his poetic instructions for mixing a salad:

> To make this condiment, your poet begs
> The pounded yellow of two hard-boil'd eggs;
> Two boiled potatoes, pass'd through kitchen sieve,
> Smoothness and softness to the salad give.
> Let onion atoms lurk within the bowl,
> And, half suspected, animate the whole.
> Of mordant mustard add a single spoon,
> Distrust the condiment that bites so soon;
> But deem it not, thou man of herbs, a fault,
> To add a double quantity of salt;
> Four times the spoon with oil from Lucca brown,
> And twice with vinegar procured from town;
> And, lastly, o'er the flavour'd compound toss
> A magic soupçon of anchovy sauce.
> Oh, green and glorious! Oh, herbaceous treat!
> 'Twould tempt the dying anchorite to eat:
> Back to the world he'd turn his fleeting soul,
> And plunge his fingers in the salad-bowl!
> Serenely full, the epicure would say,
> Fate cannot harm me, I have dined today.[10]

GRACES

The saying of grace predates Christianity. The word comes from *gratias*, the Latin for thanks. We should, no doubt, give thanks for more than food and drink, although those are the most common objects of publicly expressed gratitude. Charles Lamb said that we ought to say grace for books as well as food.

Oliver Goldsmith claimed in *The Citizen of the World* that it is the custom in China to say grace when a man goes to bed with his wife. 'Upon honour,' he wrote, 'I always find myself much more inclined to gratitude on the couch of a fine woman, than sitting down to a sirloin of beef.'

Sydney Smith had an irreverent attitude towards graces. When called upon to say them, he would look around to see if there were any champagne on the sideboard. 'O bountiful Jehovah', he would begin, if there was. If there was not, he would start, 'O Lord, even for the least of thy mercies . . .'

Smith expressed his feelings about formal graces in these terms:

> When I have sat at rich men's tables, with the savoury soup and messes steaming up the nostrils, and moistening the lips of the guests with desire and a distracted choice, I have felt the introduction of that ceremony to be unreasonable. With the ravenous orgasm upon you, it seems impertinent to interpose a religious sentiment. It is a confusion of purpose to mutter out praises from a mouth that waters.[11]

∾∾∾

There are hundreds of graces and many, like those that follow, were written to amuse rather than to be used at formal meals. Robert Herrick and Robert Burns in particular wrote several charming and celebrated graces.

> Here a little child I stand
> Heaving up my either hand.
> Cold as paddocks* though they be
> Still I lift them up to thee,
> For a benefit to fall
> On our meat and on us all.
> Robert Herrick[12]

> Some hae meat, and canna eat
> And some wad eat that want it;
> But we hae meat and we can eat,
> And sae the Lord be thank it.
> Robert Burns

* toads

The poet said this grace when visiting the Earl of Selkirk at St Mary's Isle. The Selkirk Grace is repeated by Scots all over the world on Burns Night, 25 January.

> O Lord, who made the loaves and fishes,
> Look down upon these two small dishes;
> And, though they may be exceeding small,
> Make them enough, we pray, for all;
> For if they should our stomachs fill,
> Heaven will have wrought a miracle.
> Heavenly Father, bless us,
> And keep us all alive;
> There's ten of us to dinner
> And not enough for five.
>
> 'Hodge's grace'

Grace for the Comfortably Off

> God bless this good
> Superfluous
> And may it put
> No weight on us. Amen.
>
> Frances Russell[13]

> There was once a goose and a wren
> Who gave lunch to a cock and a hen:
> 'O Lord,' prayed the goose,
> 'Bless these gifts to our use
> And ourselves in Thy service. Amen.'
>
> Anon.

> There was a young lady of Ryde,
> Who was carried away by the tide,
> A man-eating shark
> Was heard to remark,
> 'I knew that the Lord would provide!'
>
> Anon.

On china blue my lobster red
Precedes my cutlet brown,
With which my salad green is sped
By yellow Chablis down.
Lord, if good living be no sin
But innocent delight,
O polarise these hues within
To one eupeptic white!

Stephen Gaselee

When Theodore Woods was Bishop of Winchester he was once
asked to say grace before a lunch party during Cowes Week. He
noticed a storm brewing up, and prayed: 'For what we may be
permitted to retain, may the Lord make us truly grateful.'

This grace was uttered extempore by Dean Jonathan Swift after
dinner with a miser:

Thanks for this miracle! This is no less
Than to eat manna in the wilderness.
Where raging hunger reigned, we've found relief,
And seen that wondrous thing, a piece of beef.
Here chimneys smoke, that never smoked before,
And we've all ate, where we shall eat no more.

For rabbits young and rabbits old,
For rabbits hot and rabbits cold,
For rabbits tender, rabbits tough,
We thank Thee, Lord: we've had enough.

attributed to Jonathan Swift

Grace for a Cannibal Feast

Totem, votem very good showtem;
C. of E. religion not
much cop!
Fine fine dish on – boss from mission!
Plenty lousy preacher but
Good chop!

D. R. Peddy

Praise to God who giveth meat
Convenient unto all to eat;
Praise for tea and buttered toast,
Father, Son and Holy Ghost.

R. L. Gales

God of goodness, bless our food,
Keep us in a pleasant mood.
Bless the cook and all who serve us.
From indigestion, Lord, preserve us. Amen.

Anon.

I, when I undress me,
Each night upon my knees,
Do pray the Lord to bless me
With apple-pie and cheese.

Anon.

9 *At Play*

PLAY AND THE CHURCH

In considering the vocabulary of humour it has been noted that *ludicrous* comes from the Latin for play. We play for fun, but play, as is known to proverbial wisdom, is not entirely frivolous. 'All work and no play makes Jack a dull boy.' Johan Huizinga expanded on this wisdom in *Homo Ludens*, a study of the play element in culture.[1] He showed how achievements in science, poetry, philosophy, war, and in the arts, have been nourished by the instinct of play.

That instinct has been nurtured by the Church in various ways: on fields and on pitches, on courts and on courses, on tracks and on rivers. The links between sport and religion are both ancient and strong. They go back to the foundation of the Olympic Games and further. They were expressed in the much-loved and deeply religious book *The Compleat Angler* by Izaak Walton, published in 1653. Walton wrote: 'May the blessing of St Peter's Master be ... upon all that are lovers of virtue; and dare trust in His providence; and be quiet; and go a-Angling.' To write of virtue and sport in the same sentence is not absurd: the evidence is the concept of fair play.

Here can be noted some of the links between sport and the Church. Most comedy, and the best literature, arises from the more leisurely sports: those that occupy days rather than minutes or even seconds.

CLERICAL ATHLETES

Whether we find the clergy of old time generally and openly playing bowls or foot-ball – two favourite sports with the rectors and curates of the sixteenth and seventeenth centuries – or diverting themselves with games of skill and chance, which have dropped into neglect or disrepute in the present day, it is safe for us to infer that such pastimes were deemed appropriate to clergy, and that, in having recourse to them for daily recreation, ecclesiastics no more violated public decorum than the younger clergy of our time offend against prevailing opinion when they play in cricket-matches, or indulge in athletic sports. At the present date many of the ancient diversions of the English home are forbidden to ecclesiastical persons; but it is worthy of observation, that nearly every curtailment of the trivial pleasures of the clergy in one direction has been attended with corresponding extension of them in another. The Victorian rector may not play with dice, save upon a backgammon-board; but he has free leave to provide himself with a billiard-table, and try to surpass Roberts in the difficult art of making breaks. He is thought to derogate from his dignity if he drive wooden spheres over the parish bowling-green, but society is well pleased to see him play croquet on his own lawn. He may not keep hounds, but no one thinks him precluded by official obligation from lavishing money on a handsome equipage and well-filled stable.

Of the diversions still popular with our clergy, chess is one of the very few which 'the cloth' favoured in old time. In clerical biographies of the Elizabethan period, and the later days of the seventeenth century, the reader continually comes upon passages that record in language of sympathy and approval the prowess of clerical chess-players. But Baxter and other puritan divines of the Commonwealth period discerned evil in the game which prelates and deans, rectors and vicars, had played to their own delight and with the approbation of beholders from time immemorial. In 'A Letter from a Minister to a Friend concerning the Game of Chess' (1680) – a broadside preserved in the Harleian Miscellany – a conscientious and too scrupulous pastor, bewailing the faults into which an enthusiastic love of chess had betrayed him, observes, 'It hath not done with me, when I have done with it. It hath followed me into my study, into my pulpit; when I have (in my thoughts) been playing at chess: then I have had, as it were, a chess-board before my eyes: then I have been thinking how I might have obtained the strategems of my antagonist, or make such and such motions to his disadvantage; nay, I have heard of one who was playing at chess in his thoughts (as appeared by his words) when he lay a-dying . . . It hath wounded my conscience, and broken my peace. I have had sad reflections upon it, when I have been most serious. I find, if I were now to die, the remembrance of this game would greatly trouble me, and stare me in the face. I have read in the life of the famous John Huss, how he was greatly troubled for his using of this game a little before his death.'

John Cordy Jeafferson[2]

The Reverend Bute Crawley was a tall, stately, jolly, shovel-hatted man . . . At college he pulled stroke-oar in the Christchurch boat, and had thrashed all the best bruisers of the 'town'. He carried his taste for boxing and athletic exercises into private life; there was not a fight within twenty miles at which he was not present, nor a race, nor a coursing match, nor a regatta, nor a ball, nor an election, nor a visitation dinner, nor indeed a good dinner in the whole county, but he found a means to attend it . . . He rode to hounds in a pepper-and-salt frock, and was one of the best fishermen in the county.

William Makepeace Thackeray, *Vanity Fair*[3]

Rode with my elder daughter to thank Captain Possett for some grouse. He occupies Mr Hill's house at Grassenhall much to the chagrin of the old rector whose game the captain shoots. This parson is one of the old School who are nearly extinct. He plays cricket with the village lads on Sunday evenings; cuts off his own meat at the butcher's; imbibes any quantity of port and service over, descends from the pulpit, opens his pew door, offers his arm to his wife and marches out of the church before any of the congregation thinks of moving. These characters are now almost subjects of history.

Benjamin Armstrong, diary entry for 13 September, 1853[4]

Joined my family who are staying at Yarmouth. Mr Dennis Hill, a clergyman of the old school, was in the same railway carriage. He came to the station in a queer little miniature Tom Thumb sort of carriage – his own idea – drawn by a donkey. He had his double-barrelled gun with him, with plenty of carpet bags and said that he was going to a large shooting-party. Although upwards of eighty he said that he could outwalk most of the younger men and rarely missed his aim. The old veteran was clad in complete black with breeches and gaiters and was a perfect specimen of a by-gone class of clergy. With all their imperfections, however, it is impossible not to respect him.

Ibid., entry for 4 October, 1854

∾∾∾

The first boat race between Oxford and Cambridge was rowed at Henley in 1829. All eight members of the Oxford boat became clergymen, including one who became a bishop, two who became deans, and one who became a prebendary. Four members of the Cambridge crew were afterwards ordained: one bishop, one dean, one rector, and one curate.

Once in the 1950s Mrs Fisher, wife of the Archbishop of Canterbury, invited two choirboys from the cathedral to tea. Geoffrey Fisher, the

Primate, turned up later in pyjamas and dressing-gown. He said, 'I was so depressed when Oxford lost the Boat Race I went to bed.'

∾∾∾

Adrian Hastings, a Roman Catholic priest and an able historian, felt that the focus of clergymen should be on their priestcraft and was uneasy with the catholic interests of priests of the Church of England. His outlook presents a contrast to that of John Cordy Jefferson a century earlier, and to the lives of men like Henry Carrington (see p. 122).

Hastings thought that the Oxford and Cambridge Boat Race could be seen as the sacramental focus of much clerical fellowship. He wrote somewhat jaundicedly: 'The consequences of avoiding the Scylla of clericalization and the Charybdis of the secular rat race could be a life-long fixation with the boat race.'[5]

∾∾∾

The first English sports report was written by the Venerable Bede, 'Father of English History', who lived between about 673 and 735. He gave a brief report of the athletic abilities of St Cuthbert when he was a young man; he was an immensely strong wrestler and fast runner.

∾∾∾

Tennis was first played by theological students in the fifteenth century. It was taken up by both French and English royalty. The real tennis court at Hampton Court stands as visual evidence. In *Henry V*, William Shakespeare had the young king, who had received an insulting gift of tennis balls from the French Dauphin, warning the French ambassador:

> When we have match'd our rackets to these balls
> We will in France, by God's grace, play a set
> Shall strike his father's crown into the hazard.

> Tell him he hath made a match with such a wrangler
> That all the Courts of France will be disturb'd.[6]

∾∾∾

The Reverend John Thorneycroft Hartley was the Vicar of Barneston in North Yorkshire from 1874 to 1919. He was twice the Men's Singles Champion at Wimbledon, in 1879 and 1880, and runner-up in 1881. In 1879 the final was played on a Monday. Hartley did his Sunday duty in his Yorkshire parish and sat up through the night with a gravely ill parishioner, who died in the early morning. He then rode to Thirsk station and caught the train to King's Cross. A horse-drawn cab took him to Waterloo for the train to Wimbledon; in the cab he managed to change into his tennis kit. He arrived just in time to play Vere St Leger Gould in the final, beating him three sets to love.

∾∾∾

Dorothea Chambers was the daughter of Henry Douglas, Vicar of St Matthew's, Ealing Common. Had her career not been interrupted by the First World War she would surely have set an unassailable record as a Wimbledon finalist. She won the Ladies' Singles title seven times between 1903 and 1914, and played in another four finals. In 1919 she lost an epic final against Suzanne Lenglen, the score being 10–8, 4–6, 9–7. It was a clash of youth versus experience and also a celebrated contrast of fashion. The short length of Lenglen's skirt shocked the tennis world, whereas Chambers, a forty-year-old mother of two, conformed every inch to the white-stockinged Edwardian image of a lady tennis player. She met Lenglen again in the 1920 final and lost again.

Virginia Wade, who won the Ladies' Singles Championship in 1977, was also the daughter of an Anglican clergyman, Canon Eustace Wade.

∾∾∾

Several of the most famous English soccer clubs trace their ancestry back to parish church teams: Southampton (The Saints) to St Mary's; Blackpool to St John's; Bolton to Christ Church; Everton to St Domingo's Sunday School; Fulham to St Andrew's; and Queens Park Rangers to St Jude's.

∾∾∾

William Webb Ellis was an Anglican priest, the incumbent of the Church of St Clement Danes in the Strand. During a football game at Rugby School in November, 1823, when aged sixteen, he caught the ball and rushed forward with it in his arms. It made him a legendary figure as the founder of Rugby Football.

An old Rugbeian clergyman, the Reverend R. E. Inglis, was a rugby international. He was killed at the age of fifty-three bringing in the wounded under severe shell fire at the Battle of the Somme. His body was never recovered.

The first rugby match ever played in Wales, in 1856, was between a theological college and a public school: St David's College, Lampeter, versus Llandovery College, Carmarthenshire.

Twenty-two Welsh internationals were capped after their ordination as clergymen. The Reverend J. Strand Jones, who was capped in 1902 and 1903, was the first of the modern attacking full-backs. W. T. Havard, who was capped in 1919, later became the Bishop of St David's.

ANGLING

In our family, there was no clear line between religion and fly fishing. We lived at the junction of great trout rivers in Western Montana, and our father was a Presbyterian minister and a fly fisherman who tied his own flies and taught others. He taught us about Christ's disciples being fishermen, and we were left to assume, as my brother and I did, that all first-class fishermen on the Sea of Galilee were fly fishermen and that John, the favorite, was a dry-fly fisherman.   Norman Maclean[7]

September 12th Lagley, Herts ... To my old resort the trout stream, but very indifferent sport on account of their having recently cleaned out the river and dispersed the fish. Caught one fine fellow however, and lost a second after a severe struggle.   Benjamin Armstrong, *Norfolk Diary* 1876

The Fisherman's Prayer

God grant that I may live to fish
Until my dying day
And when it comes to my last cast
I then most humbly pray
When in the Lord's safe landing net
I'm peacefully asleep
That in his mercy I be judged
As good enough to keep.

                                        Anon.

Anglers, accustomed to quietness and solitude and perhaps frustration at times, possibly turn more readily to prayer than most. Here is another prayer:

Lord, grant that I may catch a fish
    So large that even I,
In speaking of it afterwards,
    May have no need to lie!

                                        Anon.

An Epitaph to a Lying Angler

He angled many a purling brook,
  But lacked the angler's skill:
He lied about the fish he took,
  And here he's lying still.

Anon.

Another angler's epitaph is to be found in the graveyard of Ripon Cathedral in Yorkshire:

Here lies poor,
  but honest Bryan Tunstall;
  he was a most expert angler
until Death, envious of his Merit,
  threw out his line, hook'd him
  and landed him here
  the 21st day of April 1790.

Epitaph

The angler rose, he took his rod,
He kneeled and made his prayers to God.
The living God sat overhead.
The angler tripped, the eels were fed.

Robert Louis Stevenson

HUNTING PARSONS

There are many stories about fox-hunting parsons. Any history of the rural clergy of England has to devote space to their hunting activities. These priests hardly uttered 'Dominus Vobiscum' before shouting 'Tally Ho!'

The Black Book, a manual of clerical decorum, stated that it was wrong for parsons to hunt in red coats. It quoted a letter from the

Archbishop of York claiming that 'provided only the *Scarlet* does not appear, the reverend successors of the apostles may leap over hedge and ditch without the slightest impropriety'.

～～～

Not all bishops were relaxed and indulgent about their hunting priests. Samuel Wilberforce, in 1846, set his candidates for ordination the following question: 'Show why indulgence in Field Sports is inconsistent with a devoted Pastoral Ministry.'

At least Wilberforce could enjoy a joke against himself. He once felt obliged to rebuke a clergyman for his addiction to fox-hunting, considering that it gave an impression of worldliness. The clergyman said that it was no more worldly than attending a ball at Blenheim Palace at which Wilberforce had been present. The bishop explained that he had been staying in the house, but was never within three rooms of the dancing. 'Oh, if it comes to that,' answered the clergyman, 'I am never within three fields of the hounds.'

～～～

Bishops themselves did not entirely escape censure about their love of this sport. Peter de Blois, Archdeacon of Bath, remonstrated with clerics addicted to sports in a folio of letters and sermons published in 1519. He particularly reprimanded an octogenarian Bishop of Rochester: 'I wish you to know that the Pope has heard that you take no care of your diocese, and pay no regard to the dignity of your office, but give up your whole life to a pack of hounds, and that age has not produced any moderation in you. My father, he says a man of eighty ought to have nothing to say to such matters, and much less a Bishop, you are bound to pursue a very different kind of hunting.'

～～～

In 1912, the elderly Reverend Charles Slingsby was thrown and killed while out hunting with the York and Aunsty Hunt. A stained glass window was later unveiled in his memory at Moor Monkton Church by the Archbishop of York, Dr Cosmo Lang, who said: 'Hunting is a sport which develops some of the finest qualities of human courage and endurance. There are many courtesies, both to man and beast, which spring naturally from the sport of the field.'

The Reverend Cecil Legard, a snobbish but enthusiastic nineteenth-century fox-hunting parson, took on the responsibility for the publication of the Fox Hound Kennel Stud Book. He would refer to heaven as 'that beautiful grass country where there's always a scent and never a blank day'. His valuable service to masters and huntsmen did not, however, prevent them from noticing his extreme partiality towards the aristocracy, and he was known amongst them as 'His Oiliness!'

> . . . Bishop Juxon, who was universally respected, not only much delighted in hunting, but 'kept a pack of hounds, and had them so well ordered and hunted, chiefly by his own skill and direction, that they exceeded all other hounds in England for the pleasure and orderly hunting of them'. Bishop Seth Ward's partiality to the same amusement is described in a most lively fashion by his biographer. 'Sometimes we by chance chopt upon the dogs, and sometimes by contrivance, knowing whereabouts they intended to hunt, but however and whensoever it happened, the bishop would ride a ring or two very briskly, but when it came to picking work, or cold hunting, he would leave them and proceed in his Promenade; but first I was sent to invite all the gentlemen to dine with him, whether he knew them or not; and this not once only, but toties quoties, as long as his health permitted.'   J. H. Overton[8]

The Reverend Sabine Baring-Gould (on whom see p. 21) recorded that when the popular clergyman Jack Russell was over eighty, he started keeping a pack of harriers. The then Bishop of Exeter sent for him.

'Mr Russell, I hear you have got a pack of hounds. Is it true?'

'It is. I won't deny it, my Lord.'

'Well, Mr Russell, it seems to me rather unsuitable for a clergyman to keep a pack. I do not ask you to give up hunting, for I know it would not be possible for you to exist without that. But will you, to oblige me, give up the pack?'

'Do you ask it as a personal favour, my Lord?'

'Yes, Mr Russell, as a personal favour.'

'Very well, then, my Lord, I will.'

'Thank you, thank you.' The bishop moved by his readiness, held out his hand. 'Give me your hand, Mr Russell; you are – you really are – a good fellow.'

Jack Russell gave his great fist to the bishop, who pressed it warmly. As they thus stood, Jack said, 'I won't deceive you – not for the world, my Lord. I'll give up the pack sure enough – but Mrs Russell will keep it instead of me.'

∾∾∾

In 1748, in spite of old age and total blindness, the Reverend Edward Stokes, Rector of Blaby in Leicestershire, rode to hounds. He was accompanied by a groom who rang a bell whenever there was a hedge to jump.

∾∾∾

The Reverend John William King (1793–1875) was the Vicar of Asby-de-la-Launde and Rector of Bassingham in Lincolnshire. In 1851 his portrait standing by his hunter – he rode with the Burton Hunt into old age – was painted by Henry Calvert. It was, however, not his hunting but his racing activities that led to a cause célèbre of the day – a dispute with Christopher Wordsworth, the Bishop of Lincoln.

King had outstanding successes on the turf. In 1874, for example, his home-bred filly Apology won three classic races – the One Thousand Guineas, the Oaks and the St Leger. The bishop unwisely used letters to *The Times* to conduct his campaign against this grand old racing vicar, who did not neglect his parochial duties and was a modest and popular figure in his parish. *The Illustrated London News* judged that 'the Right Reverend Prelate ran a poor second in the correspondence which passed between him and the aged vicar'.

∾∾∾

A story is told of an Anglican rector in a parish near Wincanton, who, when he asked a Quaker, 'Friend, which way did the hare go?' was answered: 'Friend, I cannot tell thee. But I know which way I would go if I was the hare. I would go to thy study, for I would be safe there.'

∾∾∾

The village bells chime, there's a wedding at nine,
And the parson unites the fond pair;
Then he hears the sweet sound of the horn and the
     hound,
And he knows 'tis his time to be there.
Says he, for your welfare I'll pray;
I regret I no longer can stay.
Now you're safely made one,
I must quickly be gone;
For I must go a-hunting today.
We'll all go a-hunting today,
All nature is smiling and gay,
So we'll join the glad throng that goes laughing along,
And we'll all go a-hunting today.

                           Anon.

Old Parson Beanes hunts six days of the week,
And on the seventh, he has his notes to seek,
Six days he holloas so much breath away
That, on the seventh, he can nor preach nor pray.

                           Anon.

CRICKETING CLERGYMEN

The line of celebrated cricketing parsons is a long one. It includes Frederick Beauclerk, Frank Gillingham, Edward Lyttleton, J. R. Napier, J. H. Parsons, Charles Powlett, Vernon Royal, David Sheppard and C. T. Studd. Until about 1870 almost all the Oxford and Cambridge Cricket Blues became clergymen.

The Willow and The Cloth, a compendium of cricketing clergymen from the eighteenth century has been compiled by Christopher J. Gray.[9] The length of the line can be gauged by the fact that included in this volume are the first-class, university and public school cricketing careers, as well as the ecclesiastical appointments, of fifteen hundred clergy from a single century.

> It is hard to tell where the MCC [Marylebone Cricket Club] ends and the Church of England begins.   J. B. Priestley

> It is not the mere presence of the clergy at Lords that is impressive but rather the twin stamp of English and Anglican which they bear. You can be sure they are cricketers all, and because cricket is the very soul of England it is in England's Church that they have found their vocation.
>   *Church Times*

> The English are not a very spiritual people, so they invented cricket to give them some idea of eternity.
>   George Bernard Shaw

> My wife had an uncle who could never walk down the nave of his abbey without wondering whether it would take a spin.   Lord Douglas-Home

> If Stalin had learned to play cricket the world might now be a better place to live in.
>   The Rt. Rev. R. Downey, Bishop of Liverpool, on 22 April, 1948

About 1900 a book was published privately at Stockport by Thomas Waugh, entitled *The Cricketing Faith of the Christian*. It is entirely devoted to edifying spiritual lessons drawn from the game.

∾∾∾

The Hambledon Cricket Club in Hampshire was justly the most famous club in the early history of cricket. For about thirty years this little village, miles from anywhere, was the centre of the cricket world. It was founded by the Reverend Charles Powlett who was born in 1728, a son of the third Duke of Bolton and Lavinia Fenton, the original Polly Peachum in John Gay's *Beggar's Opera*. Educated at Westminster and Trinity College, Cambridge, he became the Vicar of Itchen Abbas in Hampshire and then, in 1785, Rector of St Martin's-by-Looe in Cornwall. This new responsibility did not unduly restrict his time in Hampshire. Church registers in Cornwall reveal that he was hardly ever in the West Country. When the laws of cricket were revised at the Star and Garter Club in Pall Mall in 1774, Powlett was one of the Committee of Five. He lived on until 1809.

∾∾∾

One of the most glowing panegyrics in sporting literature was written by the Reverend John Mitford about the passing of the cricketing heroes of the Hambledon cricket club. The prose, religious in tone, has echoes of Edward Gibbon.

> Stop, reader, and look, if thou art a cricketer, with rever-
> ence and awe on that venerable and aged form! These are
> the remains of the once great, glorious, and unrivalled
> William Beldham, called for love and respect, and for his
> flaxen locks and his fair complexion, 'Silver Billy'. Beldham
> was a close-set, active man, about five feet eight inches.
> Never was such a player! so safe, so brilliant, so quick, so
> circumspect; so able in counsel, so active in the field; in
> deliberation so judicious, in execution so tremendous. It

mattered not to him who bowled, or how he bowled, fast or slow, high or low, straight or bias; away flew the ball from his bat, like an eagle on the wing. It was a study for Phidias to see Beldham rise to strike; the grandeur of the attitude, the settled composure of the look, the piercing lighting of the eye, the rapid glance of the bat, were electrical. Men's hearts throbbed within them, their cheeks turned pale and red. Michael Angelo should have painted him. Beldham was great in every hit, but his peculiar glory was the *cut*. Here he stood with no man beside him, the laurel was all his own; it was like the cut of a *racket*. His wrist seemed to turn on springs of the finest steel. He took the ball, as Burke did the House of Commons, between wind and water; not a moment too soon or late. Beldham still survives. He lives near Farnham; and in his kitchen, black with age, but, like himself, still untouched with worms, hangs the trophy of his victories; the delight of his youth, the exercise of his manhood, and the glory of his age – his BAT. Reader! Believe me, when I tell you I trembled when I touched it; it seemed an act of profaneness, of violation. I pressed it to my lips, and returned it to its sanctuary.

The last, the 'Ultimus Romanorum', we can find room to commemorate, is *David Harris*. Who knows not David Harris? the finest *bowler* whom the world ever rejoiced in when living, or lamented over when dead. Harris was by trade a potter, and lived at Odiham in Hants, an honest, plainfaced (in two senses), worthy man. 'Good David Harris' he was called; of strict principle, high honour, inflexible integrity; a character on which scandal or calumny never dared to breathe. A good cricketer, like a good orator, must be an honest man; but what are orators compared to the men of cricket. There have been a hundred, a thousand orators; there never was but one David Harris. Many men can make good speeches, but few men can deliver a good ball. Many men can throw down a strong enemy, but Harris could overthrow the strongest wicket. Cicero once undermined the conspiracy of Catiline; and Harris *once* laid prostrate even the stumps of Beldham.

It is said that it is utterly impossible to convey with the pen an idea of the grand effect of Harris's bowling. His attitude, when preparing to deliver the ball, was masculine, erect, and appalling. First, he stood like a soldier at drill, upright. Then with a graceful and elegant curve, he raised the fatal ball to his forehead, and drawing back his right foot, started off. Woe be to the unlucky wight who did not know how to stop these cannonades! his fingers would be ground to dust against the bat, his bones pulverized, and his blood scattered over the field. Lord F. Beauclerk has been heard to say, that Harris's bowling was one of the grandest sights in the universe. Like the Pantheon, in Akenside's Hymn, it was 'simply and severely great'. Harris was terribly afflicted with the gout; it was at length difficult for him to stand; a great armchair was therefore always brought into the field, and after the delivery of the ball, the hero sat down in his own calm and simple grandeur, and reposed. A fine tribute this, to his superiority, even amid the tortures of disease! . . .

We must now draw our brief memoirs to a close. Unwillingly do we drop the pen. Very pleasant has our task been, delightful our recollections. Farewell, ye smiling fields of Hambledon and Windmill Hill! Farewell ye thymy pastures of our beloved Hampshire, and farewell ye spirits of the brave, who still hover over the fields of your inheritance. Great and illustrious eleven! fare ye well![10]

∾∾∾

The Reverend Elisha Fawcett was a clergyman from Manchester, who, in the early nineteenth century, according to J. L. Carr, 'devoted his life to teaching the natives of the Admiralty Islands the Commandments of God and the Laws of Cricket. Too poor to purchase a monument to this good man, his parishioners erected his wooden leg upon his grave. In that fertile clime it miraculously took root and for many years provided a bountiful harvest of bats.'[11]

⚭⚭⚭

The Reverend Lord Frederick Beauclerk was born in 1773, the fourth son of the Duke of St Albans. He was a great-grandson of King Charles II and Nell Gwynne. He gave unutterably dull sermons from a saddle in the pulpit. Nevertheless he cut a dash when he took his stand at the wicket wearing a scarlet sash. He showed his contempt for some bowlers by suspending a valuable gold watch from his middle stump.

He was the only 'gentleman', or amateur, who was able to match the skill of the professional 'players'. He was a good example of the so-called 'shamateur'. He was said to make six hundred guineas a year from playing cricket – the equivalent of several tens of thousands of pounds today. It was rumoured that he made his fortune by backing his opponents in matches in which he himself was playing. In Soho he was known by the somewhat unclerical nickname of 'Fred Diamond Eye'.

He had a domineering personality and once persuaded the press not to publish a report of a single wicket match, simply because he had lost. The infamous and obnoxious Daniel Dawson, who was eventually hanged for horse poisoning, refused to share a carriage with him on account of Beauclerk's foul temper and even fouler language.

⚭⚭⚭

Of an entirely different mettle to his lordship was the heroic missionary Charles Thomas Studd. When he was an undergraduate at Trinity College, his magnificent batting and fielding played a large part in enabling Cambridge University to beat the Australians. He was the leading all-rounder in English cricket in 1882 and 1883. He played five times for England against Australia, but after he left Cambridge never played cricket again.

⚭⚭⚭

Frank Gillingham is pictured in *The Golden Age of Cricket* by David Frith[12] playing a ball from Wilfred Rhodes, one of the greatest of all cricketers, during an Essex v. Yorkshire match. This took place in May 1908 at Leyton in Essex, where Gillingham was a curate. He was at the microphone when the first cricket radio commentary was made in 1927. It is said that as an elderly man when preaching to his congregation he would earnestly implore them – and they included several ladies as old as himself – 'to keep their bats straight and to get their left toe out to the pitch of the ball'.

∾∾∾

Henry Foster was a clergyman of Malvern in Worcestershire. He had seven sons: Basil, Geoffrey, Harry, Johnny, Maurice, Reginald and Wilfred. Johnny, the youngest and the last survivor, died in 1978. All seven of them played for their country. Worcestershire was for a time referred to as 'Fostershire'. Reginald Foster scored 287 in his first Test Match for England against the Australians at Sydney in the 1903–4 tour. It was then the record individual Test score. Several of his brothers excelled also at other sports.

∾∾∾

The Reverend J. C. Crawford was another prolific sire of cricketers. His sons, V. F. S. Crawford, R. T. Crawford and J. N. Crawford, all became excellent county cricketers. J. N. Crawford played for Surrey and England while still in his teens. He was probably the best ever schoolboy cricketer. In 1904, after his school term at Repton, he took 44 wickets for Surrey and was virtually top of the first-class averages. In the 1907–8 series in Australia he took thirty wickets.

J. C. Crawford was an MCC committee member. He was the only objector to a motion in 1902 for the bowling crease to be increased from seventy-eight to eighty inches. He refused to give a reason for his objection – was it out of clerical conservatism or sheer bloody-mindedness?

∾∾∾

The Reverend Walter Fellows (1834–1901) has to his name the longest measured cricket drive, of 175 yards. This mighty hit was struck in 1856 on the ground of Christ Church, Oxford. Another notable hit was made about 1863 by the Reverend Francis Cornford, the Vicar of Cam. Batting on Stinchcombe Ridge in Gloucestershire, he made a stroke yielding eighteen runs. The ball was in sight all the time and thus 'Lost Ball!' could not be called out.

∿∿∿

A former Captain of England wrote of 'ballooners', balls struck which soar vertically towards the heavens. They pose a threat to the innings of the batsman, but also the hands of the fielder who has to catch them. He told the story of a clergyman who made a stupendous crack: up and up went the ball. The kindly cleric tried to comfort the fielder and himself with a few silent words. Peebles wrote:

> He afterwards confessed that in his excitement the only words which came to his mind were of a prayer for those in peril on the sea. Those he had completed thrice by the time the ball was safely held. Might it not be possible for mathematicians to compute from this data the exact height the ball did reach?   Ian Peebles[13]

∿∿∿

The cricket writer Sir Neville Cardus confessed that as a small boy he used to pray that the great batsman Ranjitsinhji would be bowled with the third ball of the next over, middle stump – he thus felt that he was giving God a reasonable margin of error.

∿∿∿

A twentieth-century sporting cleric, Canon J. R. Smith of St Mary the Virgin in Bury, is reputed to have dressed often in cricket kit beneath the canonicals and performed a marriage before joining the teams in 'the middle'.

'I haven't seen you in church for some time,' he once said to a parishioner.

'No, I'm sorry, Canon, I can't remember when.'

'I do,' said Canon Smith. 'Let me see. It was the third Sunday after Pontefract.'

&&&

An over-excited East Anglican parson immediately bowled out King Edward VII who (with immense difficulty) had been persuaded to play in a charity cricket match.

&&&

About 1879 a vicar of Eastwood in Warwickshire, having married, was told by his bride immediately after the ceremony that he could no longer use the vicarage as the cricket clubhouse.

&&&

Albert Knight, a Leicestershire County Cricket Club player and a church sidesman, customarily knelt in prayer at the crease before receiving the first ball.

&&&

The Reverend Henry Cuffin, the curate of Ruckinge in Kent, was brought before the Archdeacon's Court in 1629 for 'playing at Cricketts' immediately after divine service.

&&&

Enthusiasm for cricketing clergymen has not been universal. Bishop Samuel Wilberforce, whose disapproval of hunting parsons has already been noted, was not keen that they should take part in village cricket matches either. In 1743 the *British Champion* denounced cricket because it caused clergy to associate with the lower orders.

Archbishop William Temple (see pp. 6–7), when he was the Head-master of Repton School, once said to a group of parents: 'I have always looked upon cricket as organized loafing.' That is perhaps the most notorious flaw in the judgement of that great man.

❧❧❧

In the England v. Australia Test Match at Old Trafford in Manchester in 1956, Freddie Truman, the fiery Yorkshire fast bowler, was left out of the team. This was to allow a place for another batsman, David Sheppard, to play. David Sheppard was later to become the Bishop of Liverpool. His selection was justified; he scored 113 in England's first and only innings.

Perhaps Truman remembered his omission when Sheppard was recalled to the England team touring Australia. David's fielding and catching had slipped from his previous high standards. When he failed to stop one ball, Freddie, echoing the phraseology of the Authorized Version of the Bible, proclaimed: 'And it came to pass . . .' When David fumbled another ball in the slips, Freddie reminded him: 'You're not clasping your hands in prayer now, padre, you're trying to catch a cricket ball.'

❧❧❧

One Anglican parson was so crazy about cricket that in forgetful moments he would utter 'Over' instead of 'Amen'. He once read at the lectern and announced: 'Here endeth the second innings.' When he had a parish hall built, he had signs for the two doors, one of which said 'Out', the other 'Not Out'.

He would give sermons on the game. Three of his favourite texts were: from the Acts of the Apostles, 'Peter stood up with the eleven and was bold' (2:14); from St Paul's Second Epistle to the Corin-thians, 'I caught you by guile' (12:16); and from the First Book of Kings, '. . . drinking in the pavilions' (20:12).

❧❧❧

Letters to *The Times*:

From the Reverend David Prior:

Sir, Last Sunday I dragged myself away from watching the end of the Test match at Lord's in order to preach at our evening service on the theme of 'What Christians believe about the Trinity'. The last three balls I watched being bowled were by Ian Salisbury, England's exciting new spin bowler. The first was a leg-spinner, the second a top-spinner, the third a googly.

I had been ferreting around for a helpful illustration of the Trinity – and there it was: one person expressing himself in three different, but very similar ways. The leg-spinner's stock ball represents God the Father, who created us to 'feel after him'; the top-spinner, which goes straight through, represents the direct activity of God the Son; the googly represents the surprising activity of God the Holy Spirit.

From the Reverend R. A. Morris:

Sir, David Prior's Trinitarian illustration will have to be called wide. It reflects a serious theological error, identified in the early Church as the idea that the one God merely *acts* in different ways at different times.

Better stick to three stumps in one wicket.[14]

The Church Cricketant

I bowled three sanctified souls
    With three consecutive balls!
What do I care if Blondin trod
    Over Niagara Falls?
What do I care for the loon in the Pit
    Or the gilded Earl in the Stalls?
I bowled three curates once
    With three consecutive balls!

> I caused three Protestant 'ducks'
>   With three consecutive balls!
> Poets may rave of lily girls
>   Dancing in marble halls!
> What do I care for a bevy of yachts?
>   Or a dozen or so of yawls?
> I bowled three curates once
>   With three consecutive balls!
>
> I bowled three cricketing priests
>   With three consecutive balls!
> What if a critic hounds a book,
>   What if an author squalls?
> What do I care if sciatica comes,
>   Elephantiasis calls?
> I bowled three curates once
>   With three consecutive balls!
>
>   Norman Gale[15]

∾∾∾

The Reverend J. Dunscombe, Vicar of Sunbridge, exercised his evidently meagre poetic talent celebrating a cricket match between Surrey and Kent at Chertsey in 1773. He wrote:

> Of near three hundred notches made
>   By Surrey, eight were byes;
> The rest were balls which, boldly struck,
>   Re-echoed to the skies.

His poem ended on a moralistic note:

> God save the King, and bless the land
>   With plenty and increase;
> And grant henceforth that idle games
>   In harvest-time may cease.

∾∾∾

There was a young cleric named Grover
Who bowled twenty-one wides in an over.
    This had never been done
    By an Archbishop's son
On a Thursday, in August, in Dover.

                              Anon.

A thousand vicars prayed for a dry wicket;
When God sent rain they felt it wasn't cricket.

                              Anon.

EPITAPHS

The word 'epitaph' comes from the Greek *epitaphion* meaning 'over a tomb'. Some epitaphs were written by professionals; some were made up by friends. Often the priest or the schoolmaster was asked to provide one. Some are humorous; some are poetic. Occasionally, epitaphs can give fascinating information about conditions long ago, as well as the way people felt about things.

A good epitaph tells you at least something about the person who is immediately beneath the tomb, although it is hard to believe that anyone could be as perfect as some epitaphs suggest, hence the saying 'to lie like a tombstone'.

The following epitaphs, actual or imaginary, are all on figures of the Church. The authentic ones are almost always anonymous, but it does not follow that if they are anonymous they are therefore authentic.

᷿᷿᷿

Here lies the Venerable Wood
Lying in a box of wood,
One wood within another,
One of these woods is very good,
We're not so sure about the other.
                                   Anon.

I, the Reverend Matthew Bird,
Preacher of God's Holy Word,

Taking leave of aisle and pew,
Go to find how much is true.

L. A. G. Strong

Now rests our Vicar – They who knew him best,
Proclaim his life t'have been entirely rest.

George Crabbe

Epitaph on an Irish Priest:

Here I lie for the last time,
Lying has been my pastime,
And now I've joined the Heavenly choir
I hope I still may play the lyre.

Anon.

On Peter Robinson:

Here lies the preacher, judge, and poet, Peter,
Who broke the laws of God, and man, and metre.

Lord Jeffrey Francis

Here lies what's left of preacher Dough
He will preach no more.
For what he thought was H_2O
Was H_2SO_4

Anon.

Here Lies the Reverend Donald MacIntyre
Scottish Missionary;
Accidentally shot by his native bearer
Whilst on a missionary journey in the jungle.
'Well done, thou good and faithful servant.'

Anon.

An epitaph in Malta:

> John Tyrwitt
> A learned Divine
> He died in a fit
> Through drinking Port Wine
> April 3rd 1828, Aged 59.
>
> Anon.

> Here lies the Reverend Jonathan Doe,
> Where he has gone to I don't know:
> If haply to the realms above,
> Farewell to happiness and love;
> If haply to a lower level,
> I can't congratulate the Devil.
>
> Anon.

> His duty done, beneath this stone
>   Old Michael lies at rest,
> His rustic rig, his song, his jig
>   Were ever of the best.
> With nodding head, the choir he led,
>   That none should start too soon;
> The second too, he sang full true,
>   His viol played the tune.
> And when at last his age had passed
>   One hundred – less eleven,
> With faithful cling to fiddle string,
>   He sang himself to heaven.
>
> Epitaph of the parish clerk, Michael Turner, in
Warham churchyard, Horsham, Sussex

> Here lies interred within the stones
> The beard and flesh and eke the bones
> of Wrexham's clerk, old Daniel Jones.
>
> Dyed 1665

The trade or profession of the deceased person was often mentioned on epitaphs. At Scothorne in Lincolnshire a sexton or grave-digger is commemorated in this way:

> Alas poor John
> Is dead and gone
> Who toll'd the Bell
> And with a spade
> Dug many a grave
> And said Amen as well.

An epitaph for a sweet-smelling priest at Winchester College, dated 1541, reads:

> Beneath this stone lies shut up in the dark,
> A fellow and a priest, yclep'd JOHN CLARK.
> With earthly rose-water he did delight ye,
> But now he deals in heavenly *aqua vitae*.

Finally, here is not another ecclesiastical epitaph, but a cleric's epigram on a ducal epitaph.

In Chichester Cathedral the vault of the Dukes of Richmond is inscribed with the words: *Haec est Domus ultima* – Here is our final home.

The Reverend William Clarke, the Rector of Buxted in Sussex from 1724 to 1768, is said to have written the following epigram about this:

> Did he, who thus inscrib'd the wall,
> Not read, or not believe Saint Paul,
> Who says there is, where'er it stands,
> Another house not made with hands,
> Or may we gather from these words,
> That house is not a house of Lords?

EPILOGUES

An epilogue marks the end of a book as an epitaph does a life. In Britain the word can have a religious connotation. The last programme of the day on the radio or television is called an epilogue when it has a religious content. The following four epilogues are all book endings.

> Now pray I to them all that hear this little treatise or read it, that if there be any thing in it that liketh them, that thereof they thank our Lord Jesus Christ, of whom proceedeth all wit and all goodness; and if there be any thing that displeaseth them, I pray them also that they ascribe it to the fault of my ignorance and not to my will, that would fain have said better if I had had the wisdom.
>
> Geoffrey Chaucer

> Go, little book, God send thee good passage
> And specially let this be thy prayer
> Unto all that thee will read or hear:
> Where thou art wrong, after their help to call
> Thee to correct in any part, or all.
>
> Geoffrey Chaucer

An Epilogue

> If anything delight me for to print
> My book, 'tis this; that Thou, my God, art in't.
>
> Robert Herrick[1]

The Author to the Reader

> I've read that Luther said (it's come to me
> So often that I've made it into metre):
> *And even if the world should end tomorrow*
> *I still would plant my little apple-tree.*
> Here, reader, is my little apple-tree.
>
> Randall Jarrel[2]

SOURCES AND ACKNOWLEDGEMENTS

Every effort has been made to trace copyright ownership of items included in this book. The publisher would be grateful to be informed of any omissions.

1 · Masters of the Art

1   There are three good biographies of Sydney Smith: C. Hesketh Pearson, *The Smith of Smiths* (Hamish Hamilton, 1934); Alan Bell, *Sydney Smith* (Oxford University Press, 1980); Peter Virgin, *Sydney Smith* (HarperCollins, 1994).
2   Various collections exist of Smith's sayings, including *The Wit and Wisdom of the Rev. Sydney Smith* (Longman, Green, Longman and Roberts, 1860), from which many of the anecdotes in this book are taken.
3   Sydney Smith, *Elementary Sketches of Moral Philosophy*, Longman, Brown, Green and Longman, 1850, Lecture XI 'On Wit and Humour', Part 2, pp. 151–2.
4   Ibid.
5   Frederick Athelwood Iremonger, *William Temple, Archbishop of Canterbury. His life and letters*, Oxford University Press, 1948.
6   Alan Watts, *In My Way*, Jonathan Cape, 1973, p. 82.

2 · About the Church

1   © Alan Garner, 1971, from *The Burning Thorn*, Hamish Hamilton; used with permission.
2   Jonathan Swift, *Poetical Works*, ed. Herbert Davis, Oxford University Press, 1967.
3   Hugh Chesterman. Source unknown.
4   Sir John Squire, *Collected Poems*, Pan Macmillan, 1959. Used with permission.
5   E. C. Bentley, *The Complete Clerihews*, reproduced by permission of Curtis Brown Ltd. on behalf of the estate of E. C. Bentley, 1951.
6   Philip Larkin, *The Less Deceived*, Marvell Press: England and Australia. Used with permission.

3 · At Momentous Moments

1 *Kilvert's Diary*, Jonathan Cape, 1944.
2 Sabine Baring-Gould, *The Vicar of Morwenstow*, Henry S. King, 1876.
3 Piers Brendon, *Hawker of Morwenstow*, Anthony Molt, 1975.
4 David McCord. Source unknown.
5 F. G. Stokes, ed., *The Blecheley Diary of the Reverend William Cole*, London, 1931.
6 John Aubrey, *Brief Lives*, ed. O. L. Dick, Penguin, 1972, pp. 232–3.
7 Richard Baxter, *Works*, ed. W. Orme, 1830.
8 From the *Epigrams* of Sir John Harington (1561–1612).
9 *The Wit and Wisdom of the Rev. Sydney Smith*, Longman, Green, Longman and Roberts, 1860.
10 James Woodforde, *The Diary of a Country Parson 1758–1802*, Canterbury Press Norwich, 1999.
11 Hilaire Belloc, from 'Rebecca' in *Cautionary Tales*. Copyright permission sought.
12 Theodoret, *Collected Works*, 4 vols, Paris, 1642.

4 · At Divine Services

1 James Woodforde, *The Diary of a Country Parson 1758–1802*, Canterbury Press Norwich, 1999.
2 Clive Sansom, *Dorset Village*, Methuen, 1962. Used with permission.
3 Patrick Baker. Source unknown.
4 Woodforde, *Diary*.
5 William Ralph Inge, *Diary of a Dean: St. Paul's 1911–1934*, Hutchinson, 1949.
6 *The Memories of Dean Hole*, Edward Arnold, 1894, pp. 117–19.
7 Harley Quinn, *A Caboodle of Beasts*, Frederick Muller, 1945. Used with permission.
8 First published in the *Daily Telegraph* and used with permission.
9 Sir John Squire, *Collected Poems*, Pan Macmillan, 1959. Used with permission.

5 · In the Pulpit

1 Anthony Trollope, *Barchester Towers*, Thomas Nelson, n.d., p. 54.
2 James Boswell, *The Life of Samuel Johnson*, The World's Classics, Oxford University Press, 1980, entry for 31 July 1763.
3 W. Tuckwell, *Reminiscences of Oxford*, 2nd edn, 1907, p. 272.
4 A. E. Housman, *Letters*, Hart Davis, 1971, pp. 10–11.

5 Joseph Addison and Richard Steele, *The Spectator*, No. 112.

6 Edmund Burke, *Reflections on the Revolution in France*, ed. H. P. Adams, University Tutorial Press, n.d.

7 T. B. Macaulay, *The History of England*, J. M. Dent, 1906, vol. I, p. 365.

6 · Concerning the Clergy

1 Patrick Collinson, *The Religion of Protestants: The Church in English Society 1559–1625*, Clarendon Press, 1984, p. 101. Used with permission.

2 *The Gentleman's Magazine*, December 1734.

3 Those that follow are taken from *The Wit and Wisdom of the Rev. Sydney Smith*, Longman, Green, Longman and Roberts, 1860.

4 From Jonathan Swift, *Poetical Works*, Oxford University Press, 1967.

5 *The Diary of Sir Henry 'Chips' Channon*, Weidenfeld and Nicolson, 1967, entry for 4 April 1943.

6 John Aubrey, *Brief Lives*, ed. O. L. Dick, Penguin, 1972, pp. 231–3.

7 Richard Ingrams, *God's Apology*, André Deutsch, 1977, pp. 189–90.

8 Malcolm Muggeridge, *Diaries*, quoted in ibid., p. 237.

9 *The Wit and Wisdom of the Rev. Sydney Smith.*

10 Swift, *Poetical Works.*

11 *Echoes of the Great War: The Diary of The Reverend Andrew Clark 1914–1919*, Oxford University Press, 1988.

12 Sir Lawrence Jones. Source unknown.

13 Aubrey, *Brief Lives*, p. 233.

14 *The Times*. Used with permission.

15 *Poems of To-Day*, Sidgwick and Jackson, 1915.

16 *A Londoner's Logbook*, John Murray, 1903. Used with permission.

17 W. B. Yeats, *Selected Poetry*, ed. A. Norman Jeffares, Macmillan, 1974.

18 *The Complete Poems of Walter de la Mare*, Faber and Faber, 1969. Used with permission from the Literary Trustees of Walter de la Mare and the Society of Authors.

19 Roger Woddis. Source unknown.

20 Swift, *Poetical Works.*

21 Geoffrey Chaucer, *The Canterbury Tales*, translated into modern English by Nevill Coghill, Penguin, 1951. Copyright permission sought.

22 Anthony Trollope, *The Warden*, The World's Classics, Oxford University Press, 1980, pp. 20–1.

23 © SCM Press, 1994. Used with permission.

24 A. Tindall Hart, *The Country Priest in English History*, Phoenix House, 1959, p. 110. Copyright permission sought.

25 Simon Goodenough, *The Country Parson*, David and Charles, 1983, p. 9.

26 John Betjeman, *Collected Poems*, Faber and Faber, 1958. Used with permission.

27 S. J. Forest, *Time for a Rhyme*, Mowbray, 1957. Used with permission.

28 Mortimer Collins. Source unknown. Mortimer Collins lived between 1827 and 1876.

29 Roald Dahl, *Rhyme Stew*, Penguin, 1990. Used with permission.

30 Swift, *Poetical Works*; first published in *The Gentleman's Magazine*, December 1734.

31 *The Wit and Wisdom of the Rev. Sydney Smith*.

32 Ibid.

33 Ibid.

34 Anthony Trollope, *The Last Chronicle of Barset*, Thomas Nelson, n.d., pp. 790–1.

35 Aubrey, *Brief Lives*, pp. 387–8.

7 · In the Study

1 *The English Parson – Naturalist* (Gracewing, 2000).

2 *The Sphere*, May 1904.

3 First published in *Punch* and used with permission.

4 First published in *Punch* and used with permission.

5 Some of his autobiographical recollections can be found in *Assessments and Anticipations* (Cassell, 1929). There is a beautiful chapter about his daughter Laura in *Personal Religion and the Life of Devotion* (Longmans, Green and Co., 1924). *Vale* (Longmans, 1934) and *Diary of a Dean* (Hutchinson, 1949) are also autobiographical.

   See also the biography by Adam Fox, *Dean Inge* (John Murray, 1960).

6 George Bernard Shaw. Source unknown.

7 Humbert Wolfe, *Lampoons* (Ernest Benn, 1925). Used with permission.

8 First published in *Punch* in 1925; used with permission.

9 George Bernard Shaw, *Pen Portraits and Reviews*, Constable, 1932, p. 153.

10 Ronald Knox's niece Penelope Fitzgerald wrote about him and his brothers in a brilliant study entitled *The Knox Brothers* (Macmillan, 1977). See also Evelyn Waugh, *The Life of Ronald Knox* (Chapman and Hall, 1959).

8 · At Table

1 James Woodforde, *The Diary of a Country Parson 1758–1820*, Canterbury Press Norwich, 1999.
2 F. G. Stokes, ed., *The Blecheley Diary of Rev. William Cole*, London, 1931.
3 Anthony Trollope, *Barchester Towers*, Thomas Nelson, n.d.
4 Simon Brett, ed., *The Faber Book of Diaries*, Faber, 1989.
5 G. K. Chesterton, *Collected Poems*, Methuen, 1933. Used with permission of A. P. Watt Ltd. on behalf of the Royal Fund.
6 Oliver Sacks, *A Leg to Stand On*, Picador, 1986, p. 143. Copyright permission sought.
7 Hilaire Belloc, *Complete Verse of Hilaire Belloc*, The Nonesuch Press, 1954.
8 Jerome K. Jerome, *The Idle Thoughts of an Idle Fellow*, The Readers Library, n.d., pp. 190–1.
9 Lindsay Staniforth. Source unknown.
10 *The Wit and Wisdom of the Rev. Sydney Smith*, Longman, Green, Longman and Roberts, 1860.
11 Ibid.
12 *The Poems of Robert Herrick*, Oxford University Press, 1951.
13 Frances Russell, *Family Worship*, B. C. Hare, 1892.

9 · At Play

1 Johan Huizinga, *Homo Ludens*, Routledge and Kegan Paul, 1949.
2 John Cordy Jeafferson, *A Book about Clergy*, 1870.
3 William Makepeace Thackeray, *Vanity Fair*, Wordsworth Classics, 1993.
4 Benjamin Armstrong, *Norfolk Diary*, Hodder and Stoughton.
5 Adrian Hastings, *A History of English Christianity 1920–1985*, Collins, 1986, p. 70.
6 Shakespeare, *Henry V*, Act 1 scene 2, lines 261–7.
7 Norman Maclean, *A River Runs Through It*, University of Chicago Press, 1976, p. 1. Copyright permission sought.
8 J. H. Overton, *Live in the English Church*, Longmans, Green, and Co., 1885, p. 313.
9 This truly extraordinary work of research has a foreword by Lord Sheppard and can be obtained from The Old Rectory, Eureka via Lismore, NSW 2480, Australia.
10 Bernard Darwin, ed., *At Odd Moments*, Oxford University Press, 1941, pp. 41–3. First published in *The Gentleman's Magazine*, 1833.

11 J. L. Carr, *Dictionary of English Cricketers*, J. L. Carr, n.d.
12 David Frith, *The Golden Age of Cricket*, Lutterworth Press, 1978.
13 Ian Peebles, *Talking of Cricket*, The Sportsman's Book Club, 1955, p. 147.
14 *The Times*, June 1992. Used with permission.
15 Norman Gale, *Cricket Songs*, Macmillan and Co., 1894.

10 · At the End

1 *The Poems of Robert Herrick*, Oxford University Press, 1951, p. 376.
2 Randall Jarrel, *The Complete Poems*, Faber, 1971. Used with permission.